MEANING AND PLACE

Meaning and Place

AN INTRODUCTION TO THE SOCIAL SCIENTIFIC STUDY OF RELIGION

Hans Mol

The Pilgrim Press
New York

Library of Congress Cataloging in Publication Data

Mol, J. J.
   Meaning and place.

   Bibliography: p. 113.
   1. Religion and sociology. 2. Religion. I. Title.
BL60.M63 1983   200   82-16700
ISBN 0-8298-0638-5 (pbk.)

The Pilgrim Press, 132 West 31 Street, New York, New York 10001

CONTENTS

PREFACE

This book is geared to intelligent laypersons. It is a social scientific study, which means that all through it attempts to answer the question: What does religion do for the individual, the group, or the society? It therefore does not use the theological, philosophical, or historical approach to religion, however much it uses theology, philosophy, and history.

Each chapter begins with the description of a religious event or phenomenon, whether the Jonestown mass suicides, the Hare Krishna movement, a theological controversy in colonial America, the Islamic revival, or ancient aboriginal, Chinese, and Hindu religion. The commentary on each of these descriptions is then tied together in a more systematic conclusion at the end.

The advantage of this procedure is that the book never strays too far from concrete materials. Only at the end the pictures, accounts, and commentaries ease the reader into a more comprehensive theory about the effect of religion on the integrity of individual, group, and society. This means that this book strictly follows the inductive method: It induces or concludes from a large variety of data. Purposely, the accounts were chosen from the most diverse situations, stretching over the entire globe and over thousands of years of history. This was done to minimize both partisanship and partiality in the final conclusion.

All this makes the book the counterbalance to my *Identity and the Sacred* (Oxford: Blackwell, 1976; Book Society of Canada, 1976; New York: Free Press, 1977). That book followed the deductive method; it started out with a number of theoretical propositions that it then proceeded to elaborate. As a consequence, *Identity and the Sacred* was a rather difficult book for undergraduates and laypersons, and about 50 percent of my undergraduate classes had to read *Identity and the Sacred* three times before it all began to make sense.

I hope that by reading this book first, the students in the courses I teach in the social scientific study of religion will now have no trouble understanding the earlier book on first reading. The first draft of this study was read by my wife and my two youngest children (Margery, 16, and Gillian, 18). Whenever any of them had to read a sentence twice, she was asked to check that sentence in the margin. It was then rewritten or—more often—an extra sentence was put in to make the bridge with the preceding and following sentences clearer. I would like to thank all three of them publicly for their contribution to making this book more readable.

Also, in contrast with *Identity and the Sacred,* no references were used. The clutter of citations in the earlier book affected its readability adversely. If the reader wants to have further references to the materials here presented, he or she will find a list of books and articles at the end of this volume that will aid in tracing the sources. More often than not, however, the thinking of this book goes beyond my previous work. I like to think of my work as constantly developing and maturing and therefore ever improving on previous efforts.

MEANING AND PLACE

CHAPTER 1

Place

Some scholars say that the religion of the Australian Aborigines is the oldest and the simplest. Others question the observation. Whatever the case, it is certainly *one* of the oldest and simplest. What are its main features?

Territory is fundamental to Aboriginal life and religion. It is a precious commodity. It is the sole source for sustaining life. Yet it is often desertlike and desolate, and this is all the more reason to treat it with circumspection and reverence, it seems. Before white persons settled in Australia, in 1788, the Aborigines eked out a precarious existence by hunting animals and gathering plants, roots, and insects. Few natives still live this way, and this short account of their religion is therefore mainly a reconstruction of those Stone Age days.

Is it actually true that the land was revered in the same way as underlings grovel before a despot? Certainly the Aborigines were completely at the mercy of their environment. Scholars who follow Karl Marx and Sigmund Freud are inclined to think about religion as a debasement before a tyrannic father figure or as frantic appeasement of forces, such as drought, death, disease.

Yet the evidence of Aboriginal religion goes against this view of religion. Aborigines, like many other natives in other countries, do not think of themselves as standing over against nature. Separation of the self from group or group from nature is a rather recent development. Aborigines identify with nature and feel at one with the mountain range formed by the boomerang of mythical ancestors or the creek shaped by their dancing feet or the waterholes still showing their footprints. To Aborigines, the entire landscape is peopled with traces of mythical beings, all very much alive and all intricately interwoven with everyday living. Landscape and life are basically one. However tragic drought, death, and disease they do not nullify order. And this seems to be the hub of Aboriginal religion: identification with the indissoluble order of nature and society.

It begins at birth. Conception is located in the features of nature. A spirit child is hidden in the rock where the mother was resting or in the animal or plant she was eating. This spirit child is to have entered her at this location and begun the pregnancy. Often this location or the animal or plant becomes the personal emblem (or totem) of the infant because of its association with the first stirring in the womb. And so individuals are tied to the earth and derive their identities from specific items in the landscape. Sometimes Aborigines point to various marks on their bodies (for instance, warts or patches of different skin color) as being the same as the marks on the rocks where the spirit children entered their mothers' wombs.

Nonpersonal, social emblems are similarly linked with nature. The integrity of the smaller clan or the larger tribe (consisting of a number of clans) increases with the common identification with the totem peculiar to each, whether an opossum, a white ant, the desert pea, or even water. The emblem unifies the membership and therefore constant attention is drawn to it through scrupulous avoidance or through the central place it occupies in the corroborees (rituals) and myths.

A tribe then has a distinct geographical boundary. It occupies a well-delineated, secure place in an environment that becomes increasingly more threatening, strange, and unfamiliar the farther one moves away from it.

Yet this place also has a social boundary generally coinciding with the geographical one. The members are bound together by the common totem that separates them from other tribes with other emblems. In the same way as the landscape is filled with revered ridges, gullies, and the familiar plants and animals, so the tribal society is filled with a variety of individuals and groups all standing in orderly, well-recognized relation to one another. Everything has its place in both nature and society.

The security of both the geographical and social order is enhanced by attitudes of reverence. Outside this secure order Aborigines feel hopelessly lost and lonely. They feel endangered and sometimes paralyzed with fear in the territories of other Aborigines with other totems, other languages, and other ancestors.

Yet order, whether physical or social, is always precarious. Bushfire and flood, famine and death undermine physical existence. Cunning is not sufficient for survival. Calamities must be contained or absorbed back into ordered structure. Survival therefore dictates interpretation, because it alone can relate accidents of life and nature to order. And so the Arunta in Central Australia take the sting out of death through reiterating the stories of an ageless skyworld, where there are no droughts and where the Milky Way flows like a broad river with the campfires of the skydwellers on the banks.

Elaborate death rituals in all Aboriginal societies guide the transition to normality. It is as though the deceased has left a tear in the social fabric that the rituals then carefully, slowly, yet persistently, mend.

There are many other threats to the social fabric. Tension between individuals, between the sexes, and between individual and group can be highly disruptive. And insofar as religion through the totem reinforces each major unit of social organization or "identity" (personhood, womanhood, malehood, and tribe) it may deepen rather than modify the disruption. And so the group may use religion to strengthen its stance against obstinate individuals, such as the father of famous Aboriginal painter Albert Namatjira, in Central Australia. He eloped with a girl from the "wrong" kin-group class, thereby challenging the established tribal order. For punishment he was not only speared in the thigh, but also excluded from instruction by his elders into the sacred tradition of his own conception site, the flying ant totemic center of Intalua. In other words, the group attempted to diminish his personal identity by withholding the sacred information that otherwise would have strengthened it.

Totems have also been used to clarify conflicts between the sexes. In a certain tribe in New South Wales the killing of a bat (the totem of manhood) by the females (whose totem was a particular bird) signified open conflict. By killing the bird the men could and did retaliate.

Aboriginal religion is not just confined to totemic ceremonies. In a variety of tribes totems are the concrete, specific representations of a larger order, translated into English as The Dreaming. Yet to think of The Dreaming as "abstract" is doing it an injustice. It combines many items that the Western mind strictly separates: reality, symbol, body, spirit, totem, spirit-site.

It closely hovers over, encompasses, person and totem—making them inseparable. It is the dynamic creation of oneness and unity that is also typical for dreams. Dreams, too, absorb disorder by reordering and reorganizing images, patterns, and events. And so The Dreaming delineates order, thereby minimizing the unpredictable in Aboriginal society and maximizing the management of a precarious existence.

COMMENTARY

So far I have only summarized the main features of Aboriginal religion. Any summary or description also interprets, but now I must be somewhat more systematic in my interpretation. Under which headings can we now look at Aboriginal religion so that the account coheres in a social scientific way? Let us try these three subheadings: (a) geographical and social place, (b) kinds of identity and their conflict, and (c) religion as the reinforcer of identity.

a. Geographical and Social Place

We have seen how territory was intricately interwoven with religion and life of the Aborigines. Why was it so important?

In a harsh environment only those who know how to use the scarce resources will survive. And so detailed familiarity with the environment becomes a necessity. Again and again in Australia white travelers perished in the dry inland where the natives had lived all their lives, because only the latter knew which roots contained potable water and which plants were edible.

In addition, scarce resources can be shared only with a limited number of others. Aborigines were and are in this respect no different from birds and other animals who keep intruders out of their territories by such "no trespassing" signs as bird calls and scents or, if these do not help, by attack.

Humans have other advantages in the creation of a secure niche in the environment: tools and cooperation. Elementary forms of tools (twigs for retrieving honey out of a bee's nest, for instance) were used by some apes. And workers and soldiers cooperate in ant colonies. Yet humans could develop these means of dealing with the environment much more extensively. Signs developed into symbols and symbols developed into language because tribes possessing these intricate means of communication could deal more effectively with the environment. Social solidarity, mutual cooperation, and communication outdid individual prowess as a means to master nature. Hand in hand with this improved control went an increasingly more complex division of labor. Even as primitive a society as the Aboriginal one could hunt and defend itself more effectively than groups of animals, because it could pass on knowledge about tools and could cooperate in foraging and fighting, each person contributing what he or she was best at.

Yet in contrast with modern society, geographical and social place were at one in Aboriginal society. Without its territorial base the clan or the tribe was nothing. This is still largely true for a nation or a community in this day and age, but it is not true for families, clubs, sects, companies, individuals, and other units of social organization. They can move to other locations without much damage to their integrity.

For the sake of greater economic security people have become much more mobile and much less attached to local roots. This means that geographical place has receded as the major pivot around which security revolves. Yet even the most cosmopolitan of citizens are aware that rootlessness has its own psychological price and that mobility can undermine the cohesion of family and community. And so families may refuse to move to other parts of the country where employment opportunities are better or employees forego promotion if that means migrating to other branch plants.

Humankind has moved far from the frantic fears of the Aborigines who found themselves in nontribal territory. And yet they too cannot live as chameleons, constantly adjusting to new environments. The emptiness, rootlessness, and meaninglessness that have accompanied technical progress have put a premium on a sense of belonging, a sense of place in a stable community. Modern men and women, too, require boundaries around their integrity, a safeguard for their traditions, and the security of roots. This they have very much in common with their Aboriginal forebears.

All this means that technical progress, a very intricate division of labor or, as it is sometimes called, "differentiation" (a continuous specialization of tasks, fragmentation, putting a premium on innovation and "unlikeness"), does not reign unchecked. It is limited by humankind's need for place and identity, whether geographical or social. It is curbed by humankind's preference for sanity and wholeness when these are endangered by too much change.

The other side of the coin must also be mentioned. The entrenched sense of place and fear of anything beyond the familiar boundaries of tribal territory made the Australian Aborigines so vulnerable to change that their world caved in when the white settlers arrived. Tradition, roots, the sanctity of the soil, an encrusted meaning system can also endanger survival. Integration (a binding together, a maintaining of sameness, an abiding concern with wholeness, unity, and order) can minimize change to such an extent that viability is lost irretrievably.

Comparing Aboriginal and modern Western society I therefore conclude that in a surviving society a sense of place and identity is held in check by the human need for mastery, economic independence, and technical progress. And the other way round: Change or differentiation is held in check by the need for stability or integration. They seem to be the basic, countervailing forces in existence, now pulling toward more change, now counterpulling toward more stability, according to which is on the upper side on the seesaw or winning the tug-of-war. If either of these forces has too much of an upper hand in a particular society, doom is imminent. Evolution favors a roughly equal balance. A dialectic (a conflicting and yet complementing relationship between two opposing forces) between differentiation and integration therefore appears to determine the survival of any civilization.

b. Kinds of Identity and Their Conflict

Aboriginal society was the result of environmental pressures. Without protection by the group, neither infant, mother, nor warrior could have survived. The quality of the protection in turn depended on group solidarity. The greater the cohesion, the better the chances of survival of both individual and group. The kind of help one could rely on in times of trouble depended on the strength of the whole, not the individual, however brave, strong, or skillful.

Yet to maximize social solidarity, all sorts of sacrifices had to be made. Basic instincts of aggression had to be suppressed where they would harm the social whole and encouraged where they would strengthen solidarity. And this meant that from an early age children had to learn restraint and self-control as well as cunning and force, according to the situation.

For the sake of the social whole, the very simple rule of every individual for himself or herself had to be replaced by a carefully constructed consensus about goals, rules of distribution of prey, rights of access to women, conformity to values. And all this meant more coordination, greater sensitivity toward others, and above all, a more complex social organization.

The totem—and the various rituals that went with it—embodied or represented this complex social whole and became a sort of shorthand for the underlying unity, or what held the complexity together. Anthropologist Linton describes how very similarly in World War I the rainbow became the rallying point for the 42d Division of the American Expeditionary Force, to which he belonged. Here, too, the rainbow summed up the diversity of people, races, and regions making up the unit.

Just as an army corps has subunits to which soldiers feel loyal (sometimes even more loyal), so the Australian Aborigines had smaller bands or clans making up the larger tribe; they had their own totems. Other units of social organization, such as womanhood, manhood, moieties (usually the exogamous half of a tribe or the half providing the marriage partners for the other half), and individuals, were similarly represented by various emblems. These "identities" did not always harmoniously intertwine, if only because social restraint and personal self-affirmation—like repression and expression—do not go together very well. Aboriginal initiations are a good illustration of the ordeal inflicted on adolescents in order to strip them of their carefree boyhood identities and weld them to responsible manhood.

Similar examples of identity conflict can be found in modern societies. During World War II I happened to be an inmate in a variety of German penal establishments. The Germans felt rather strongly that my Dutch friends and I broke down the German social order by our subversive activities, such as listening to the BBC and discussing the British version of the news with whoever wanted to listen. I in turn felt that my personal integrity or wholeness was undermined by the German assumption that I would fit in the German order. In other words, two centers of wholeness (my personal identity and the German social one) clashed, and I was actually very lucky that I survived that conflict, because the Germans did not particularly care whether the unexploded bombs they made us dig out went off or not.

Now totems in the case of Australian Aborigines or beliefs in the case of my clash with the Nazis strengthen the coherence of each separate identity. If the German nation had not been held together by strong beliefs in its supremacy, the *Blut und Boden* theology, and the godlike qualities of the Führer, it would have disintegrated even before D-day. And consequently, my survival chances would have been much, much better.

And the other way round: If I had not had such a strong belief in the necessity for independent inquiry, the supremacy of truth, and the democratic process, the Germans would have found me much, much less obnoxious than they did. In other words (and here I come to the crux of the matter), the beliefs had a decided effect on both coherence and the breakdown of that coherence. They made both the Germans and me much more determined than we otherwise would have been. Yet precisely because these beliefs were so clearly established and delineated, the clash did become a matter of life and death. Understand me well—not just for me, but also for the Germans. If they had not been so keen to protect their ideology, they would have succumbed much earlier to both the allied armed might and the determination of a subversive underground.

This point about religious items, such as beliefs strengthening a variety of identities, is elaborated in the following section. Here it remains to make the point that both in the most ancient as well as in the most modern societies one can observe a variety of identities on a variety of levels, such as social (national, tribal), group (clan, adulthood, community, family, club, sect, etc.), and individual. The whole and the parts may not be well attuned to one another in modern dynamic societies: Individuals may be at cross-purposes with their families, and families may demand loyalties that the state (e.g., in communist China) wants to usurp. Yet however much conflict or congruence there may be, it is important that each unit of social organization is analyzed as such and not just as a derivation of the individual. The effect of religion can only be understood if we relate it to a variety of identities rather than one, as happens much too often in the scholarly literature.

c. Religion as the Reinforcer of Identity

As said earlier, in Aboriginal society major units of social organization, such as tribe, moiety, clan, manhood, womanhood, person, are strengthened in a variety of "religious" ways.

1. First of all, the totem or emblem sums up, or is a shorthand term for, the unit in question. If the wallaby (a small kind of kangaroo) is the totem, the tribe thinks of itself as a wallaby. Being a wallaby distinguishes it from the neighboring tribe, which might be a bandicoot.

The totem orders through delineation, and The Dreaming that comprises the totem orders through absorbing and arranging events and images. The Dreaming represents the unity of experiencing and organizing that experience.

If this process of ordering can be called objectification

(making order into an object), it is a most embryonic form of this process. Object and subject are not distinguished. They belong together. An individual is part of The Dreaming and does not stand aside from it. And yet The Dreaming orders and thereby modifies the unpredictable and ordinary. It gobbles up the crassly capricious as the white blood corpuscle gobbles up the invading germ. It immunizes the whimsical. There is no distinction between the imagined and the real, the spiritual and the actual.

Yet there *are* distinctions between one tribe and another or one clan and another or one individual and another. Or to use the words from section (a): Society had become differentiated, units had become separated out. Separate functioning, coordination between relatively independent units allowed a more complex whole to deal more effectively with the environment. Still this differentiation was embryonic compared with the proliferating diversity of industrial society, where segments of persons (roles) rather than individuals often form the cement.

2. Second, identities are also reinforced by loyalties, commitments, emotions. In Aboriginal society there is no room for the aloof outsider. Solidarity is mainly a matter of strong sentiments of loyalty. Any hesitation or reservation about these feelings of dedication to the group will weaken its capacity for unified action. And this capacity for unified action is precisely what gives the clan or the tribe the crucial edge in the battle for survival in a precarious environment.

Sacrifices of blood in the totemic ceremonies are forms of dedication to clan identity at the expense of the diminishing self. Self-denial or abstinence (particularly at times of initiation) strengthened Aboriginal manhood. Through these acts the initiate would show his commitment to his new identity for all to see.

In Aboriginal society there are also strong feelings of dread in the face of taboos. Many of these taboos deal with eating the animal or plant totem. Indirectly, through dread, the outline of clan organization is reinforced. In certain tribes the prohibition of certain desirable foods is relaxed according to age, and in this way the age hierarchy is reinforced. Old age becomes a desirable status under this system.

It is not necessary to describe similar feelings of loyalty pervading the most advanced society. The absence of such feelings (e.g., the dread Americans experience when radicals burn the flag) is often explained as a serious undermining of national sentiment. Similarly, the capacity to die for one's gang in gang warfare is a modern example of religious commitment to a particular group identity. The essential difference between Aboriginal and modern society should not be overestimated.

3. Ritual is a third way to strengthen identities or major units of social organization. By acting out the gait and movement of the totem animal the clan reenacts its own fundamental being. The performing members of the wildcat clan trail a long grass cord, imitating the animal's tail. The men of the emu clan wear headdresses suggesting the long neck and beak of the emu, while patterns of down are glued to their skins with human blood.

Rites of passage (such as birth, marriage, and in Aboriginal society, particularly initiation and death rituals) guide the transition from one identity to another. Initiation ceremonies illustrate the principle behind rites of passage: the stripping of one identity (boyhood) and the welding of a new one (manhood). Death rites guide the changeover from a disrupted group to a reintegrated one. The greater the gap left by the deceased, the more elaborate the burial rites tend to be.

Again the basic similarities in rites between the most ancient tribes and modern society is striking. We have all participated in rites of passage, and even the most avowedly secular societies (for instance, communist nations) have instituted secular initiation, marriage, and death rituals. Any nation state worthy of its name has flag-raising ceremonies and memorial marches for those who gave their lives in wars of the past. And in all instances these ceremonies lend greater dignity and solemnity to the national identity.

4. Myths represent yet another way to buttress geographical or social place. Many Aboriginal myths deal with features of the landscape. They are told repeatedly and thereby fix patterns of interpretation in the mind. The unadulterated horror of the bushfire becomes associated with the chase of two firesticks that two brothers—Kambi and Jitabidi (living in the sky near the Southern Cross)—had left behind while on an opossum hunt. Being bored with nothing to do they begin to pursue each other, upon which the grass catches fire. The brothers return at once, gather the firesticks, and journey back to the sky.

Like the myths that modify the stark forbiddingness of nature into something created intentionally, so the moral myths soften the impact of social tension by relating it to what the ancestors did. Many of these myths deal with sexual injury and illicit sex, as these were often the underlying causes of communal discord. A particular star in the Orion constellation is pointed out as originally being the penis of an indiscreet ancestor, which was forced to lead an independent existence after being bitten off by the dogs of the woman it had hurt.

A common theme in many myths is the transition from one phase (through separation or being swallowed or killed) via a phase of resting inside the skybeing, python, or demonic woman, to another phase (being revived, regurgitated, reanimated). These myths all dramatize the emergence of a new wholeness from the breakdown of an old one. There is a similarity here with a major theme running through Christian theology: that salvation (wholeness) has been or must be rescued from the clutches of sin (chaos, breakdown). In both cases the theme is relevant to basic experiences of people, whether living under the most primitive conditions or sheltered by the affluence of modern culture. In both cases humankind's place (whether geographical or social) is made more habitable through the wider context in which order and chaos are located.

CHAPTER 2

Meaning

On January 31, 1720 a young minister by the name of Theodorus Jacobus Frelinghuysen preached his first sermon in the Dutch Reformed Church of Raritan, New Jersey. He had just arrived from the Netherlands, and many of his parishioners soon wished that he had never left the place. He insisted on barring the unconverted from the communion table. Only those who repented their sins and showed a desire to mend their ways should be members of the church, he said.

An ugly, ever-widening controversy arose, polarizing the Dutch clergy in the New York/New Jersey area into two hostile camps. On the one side were Frelinghuysen and three other ministers, ardent in their evangelical beliefs. On the other side were the six orthodox clergymen who defended traditional, formal theology. The Evangelicals felt no qualms at splitting churches and families into the converted and the unconverted. The orthodox, however, made religious issues secondary to family and congregational harmony. The Evangelicals roamed far and wide to make or meet converts without bothering much about national origin. The orthodox insisted on keeping things in the Dutch way. The Evangelicals had no compunction about cutting ecclesiastical ties with the mother country. The orthodox were loath to start an independent church organization in the colonies.

The controversy lasted for decades. By and large the orthodox lost out and the Evangelicals went from strength to strength. Frelinghuysen and his close friend Gilbert Tennent became the forerunners of the Great Awakening (religious revivals), which swept the American colonies later in the eighteenth century.

A rather similar split existed in the German Lutheran Church. Here the Evangelicals (or Pietists) were grouped around Henry Melchior Muhlenberg in Pennsylvania, and the orthodox, around Wilhelm Christophorus Berkenmeyer in New York. The Muhlenberg group made rules and church organization depend on what was most helpful to convert people, and this meant considerable lay participation. By contrast, the Berkenmeyer group insisted on following the German, more authoritarian rules to the letter.

The Pennsylvania Evangelicals mixed rather happily with the English at revival meetings. The New York orthodox kept aloof from all others. Muhlenberg solved the bitter language controversies in the New York Lutheran Church, which had started in the 1740s, by preaching in English and German as well as in Dutch, which had begun to wane as the common language of the region.

The New York orthodox relied on ministers from Europe and were not interested in recruiting and training candidates locally. Muhlenberg and the other Pietists in Pennsylvania began to train a native ministry and ordain local candidates. The Berkenmeyer organization failed miserably. The flexible Muhlenberg organization took over and succeeded, despite the fact that its base (the German belt of Pennsylvania) was more homogeneously German than New York ever was.

The same situation prevailed in the Presbyterian churches: The orthodox insisted on keeping things Scottish; the Evangelicals denationalized religion. Wherever the revivals of the Great Awakening took place (in the second half of the eighteenth century), ethnic and class barriers tended to be modified. And wherever local churches attempted to preserve Scottish or English culture, they tended to become isolated.

COMMENTARY

a. Meaning and Order

One often hears the term search for meaning. What does it mean and how does it relate to the eighteenth century controversies?

Search for meaning is the search for an order to which one can relate experiences and events. It is part of the human attempt to avoid too many surprises and unforeseen circumstances. The Dutch in New York in the early 1700s found in their religion the security of the familiar language, the familiar ritual, a reinforcement of customary ways of acting and reacting, a strengthening of values of sturdiness and responsibility, and a confirmation of their own social position.

Frelinghuysen and his followers seemed to undermine the very foundations of stability to a considerable number of Dutch laypeople and elders who helped to draw up the 246 pages of the *Complaint* (1725) to the authorities in the Netherlands about the behavior of the Evangelicals. Instead of protecting an increasingly precarious "Dutchness" (more and more English began to settle in an area that had been taken from the Dutch in 1664), these fervent preachers of conversion seemed to be less interested in a God who protected the Sainted country, their families, and their class than a God who seemed to be exclusively interested in the state of a person's soul and in his or her conversion from sin.

"Meaning," to the New York and New Jersey Dutch in the first quarter of the eighteenth century, was the frame of reference provided by the Dutch Reformed Church insofar as it supported their hopes, their actions, and their values and insofar as it accounted for disease, death, and disaster. "Meaning" was the coherent and consistent relation not only between the things that were right, but also the things that were or had gone wrong. "Meaning" had to do with the wholeness of their most crucial identities, whether family, community, country, occupation, or their personal places.

As with the Australian aborigines, these various identities were connected. Yet there were also crucial differences. For one, family identity was much stronger. For another, the independence of the individual had now become firmly established. For a third, the system of "meaning" had now become objectified.

What do we mean by "the system of meaning had now become objectified"? In aboriginal religion The Dreaming and the totems, as we have seen, hovered so closely around every act and event that they were looked on as identical to all intents and purposes.

By contrast, in the religion of the Dutch Reformed, the order in terms of which every act and event was seen was separated from these acts and events. The "spiritual" had become differentiated (separated out from) the "ordinary." God ruled on high. God's rule was vitally relevant. Yet God's eternity, omnipotence, and omniscience were not in any way to be confused with humankind's temporality, little power, and knowledge.

God's holiness stood in contrast with humankind's lapse from grace. Only God could save those who had sinned. In other words, wholeness was not in humans, but in God. By contrast, dissolution was characteristic of humans, only suspended through faith in God's infinite goodness and love.

In other words, order for the Dutch Reformed was objectified (made into a separate object) in God. It was God who towered above the world, God's handiwork. In God rather than in humans did the strands come together. Yet humans could participate in this order, by proxy as it were. Faith was the all-important link. Through obedience, loyalty, and commitment, humans could be tied to God, who had created order out of chaos and who had made Jesus Christ whole again after his body was broken on the cross. Humans, too, could be made whole again through God's gracious act.

There were both social advantages and problems with the objectification of God in Calvinism. The benefits are particularly clear when compared with the aboriginal way of summing up order and unity in The Dreaming. The evolutionary advantage of differentiation in all spheres is the separating out of those items that can be more usefully done separately. By fusing order and disorder, the sacred and the ordinary, the spiritual and the real so closely together in The Dreaming, aboriginal society became rather inflexible.

By separating these spheres so that their relationship would less hamper adaptation (the fitting of humans in a changing environment), humans became freer to manipulate and master nature. A more advanced technology, economy, polity, and science are not possible when the existing technology, economy, polity, and science are regarded as untouchable and sacred.

The Dreaming made everything whole. And this was precisely what gave aboriginal society the capacity to cope with its particular social and physical environment. Yet it made the whole so inflexible that aboriginal society proved to be incapable of adaptation when white people arrived on the scene.

By contrast, the white people's religion had separated out (differentiated) those elements in the whole that could be manipulated without squeamishness (the mundane, worldly) from those elements that preserved order (the sacred, otherworldly). Of course both spheres, now separated out, needed each other, and this is why I have termed the relationship "dialectic," as the ordinary and the sacred were opposed and yet in need of each other. They were opposed just as stability is opposed to change. Yet they needed each other. Stability can lead to inflexibility if any change is precluded. Change without stable goals can destroy everything in its path.

Yet despite the advantage of Christianity in this respect, there are disadvantages as well. They are illustrated by two problems faced by orthodox Calvinists. By objectifying God so much (even good works had been rejected as a potent, strengthening interconnection), the faith or commitment link had to carry the entire burden of the God/human relationship. Later it proved to be rather easily snappable, with the result that secularization has tended to follow Calvinism.

The second problem was the Calvinist underestimation of the consolidating potential of any religion for units of social organization. Frelinghuysen's opponents had settled into a routine that interlocked church, family, community, and individual. The faith had become embedded in the status quo. It became identified with Dutch aspirations, prosperity, comforts, and patterns of upbringing. It certainly did not challenge them seriously. And so while nothing had changed in the conceptualization of God, in actual fact God had become the safe guarantor of a specific time and place.

b. Meaning and Change

Frelinghuysen and his band of Evangelicals were not in any way less Calvinistic than their opponents. However much the latter tried, they did not succeed in convincing the ecclesiastical arbiters in Amsterdam that the Evangelicals were heretics. The church court of the Netherlands only disapproved of Frelinghuysen admitting an English dissenter (they meant Gilbert Tennent) to pulpit and sacraments, which act they regarded as a neglect of Dutch Church Order.

The real rub lay in the fact that the very institution of society that dealt with the essence of order tended to undermine this order by introducing new distinctions (converted versus nonconverted) as more fundamental. For this reason the religious controversies were so bitter: They dealt with people's basic security.

Yet these new criteria were in no way unscriptural or contrary to Reformed theology. It was extreme evangelical seriousness about conversion as compared with the benign neglect by the orthodox that caused the trouble.

Why was this stress on conversion regarded as so deadly?

It assumed that there was a drastic need for change when in actual fact most of the Dutch Reformed were fairly well satisfied with the way things were. It was easy enough to think of sin as a detectable aberration. Morals always needed support. It was something quite different to think of sin as a basic flaw of one's innermost being that could be repaired only by divine intervention. Not that the orthodox layperson did not pay lip service to this theological point of view. After all, it was standard Calvinism. However, Frelinghuysen and his group insisted that one actually had to feel deeply the intolerable burden of the flaw in order to experience its opposite:

being united with the Savior and being miraculously restored to wholeness.

Conversion meant to the Evangelicals that one was emotionally stripped of one's flaw or brokenness and that one was emotionally welded to a new identity. Yet what to do if in all honesty one could not even fake the terror of being squashed by sin? This was the situation in which the "unconverted" parishioners of Raritan had found themselves. Or also fellow clergymen Du Bois and Boel of the New York region, who had been singled out as being "unregenerated." Embarrassment was the source of concerted antagonism.

Why then did the Evangelicals of any stripe (Dutch, German, English, American) win the day in the latter half of the eighteenth century? The Great Awakening certainly brought many sinners to Christ all over the country and particularly on the expanding North American frontier.

One answer is that in a nation of relatively recent, struggling settlers old identities tended to become obsolete, and new identities, to be at a premium. The picture of the relatively self-satisfied Dutchman, happy with himself, his family, and his occupational prospect is certainly overdrawn. Deviance, crime, alcoholism, and gambling were rife in many communities. Loose morals ruined many a family.

The American frontier tended to draw the marginal individual, the kind of person who could not make a go of it in his or her place of origin. Often this person was a social misfit. Even if adventure or tales of economic opportunity had been the motive for migration, the new settler tended to be less entrenched emotionally in the community which was found easy to leave. The settler was often a loner and suspected of being a nonconformist at heart.

Yet when these pioneers began to be successful in the proliferating new settlements, their increased sense of responsibility for their families, farms, and budding communities gave them a new outlook. The new wholeness in Christ promised by the roving preachers seemed to be a fitting capping stone for people whose pasts were filled with remorse and guilt. To accept God's forgiveness and offer for salvation was to get a new lease on life. Numerous are the detailed accounts of sin that the converted would confess with great contagion to the rapt revival audiences. They were all genuine, because each of these sinners had experienced what it meant to be rotten to the core and to be splendidly renewed by the cleansing blood of Christ.

The success therefore of Evangelicals, such as Frelinghuysen, and of Pietists, such as Muhlenberg, lay in the fact that their message of redemption and conversion fitted an age of rapid change. They and the leaders of the great revivals were charismatic preachers who galvanized audiences and welded new enthusiastic communities of converts. They catered to the large mass of people who were searching for new meaning and new identities. The strong impact of the Great Awakening in North America (as compared with the lesser effect of its European origins) lies in the sectarian capacity for welding new identities out of obsolete old ones.

The irony was that the succeeding generations were less in need of further testimonies to profound religious experiences and more in need of the consolidation and maintenance of the existing identities (whether personal, family, communal). And so fervent sectarianism turned into sedate ecclesiastical form. The children of Frelinghuysen's converts became frighteningly similar to his erstwhile opponents, unless of course they had gone through an acute rebellion against their parents' religiosity, which gave them something to feel profoundly guilty about.

The main point of this section, however, is that the Christian frame of reference (God's order) was capable of dealing not only with the consolidation of identity (this was the point of section [a]), but also with its destruction when that became necessary. The controversies resulted not from the inadequacy of Christian theology to deal with both order and change, but from the thoroughly diverse functions that the parishioners came to expect from religion.

In the same way as in the past the "spiritual" had become separated out (differentiated) from the "mundane," so within the spiritual, the sectarian, evangelical mode became separated out from the churchlike, orthodox, or later liberal, mode. It was by means of this differentiation that each function could better come into its own.

A related point is that independence of the Christian frame of reference (God's order), untrammeled by the confusions of the here and now, gave it the leverage for judgment of the mundane. Ever since, a religious ethic has felt free to advocate closer congruence with its own independent set of principles. God's order is not just a reflection of humankind's need for order or change; it is also the producer of standards by which the mundane is judged. The prophetic call to turn from evil has generally been a potent reminder to succeeding generations of the West as to which direction they should move if a divine blueprint were the charter.

c. Marginality, Adjustment, Capitalism, Democracy, and Science

I have to elaborate my point in the previous paragraph that the Christian frame of reference, as interpreted by the eighteenth-century Evangelicals, provided a leverage for change.

God's order was the point of reference that gave meaning to the acts and events in which the individual and his or her family and community were involved. It therefore strengthened these identities, or to say it in sociologese, it strengthened the boundary-maintaining systems of personality, kinship, and society. This was the argument of section (a). If the human muddle and mess can be related to order, then the muddle and mess are "relativized," or to say the same differently, the muddlement and "messness" become less so; they are modified.

Yet the very independence of an all-powerful predestining, foreordaining God, as staunch Calvinists believed, "relativized" also in a different fashion. It lessened the attachments to families, communities, countries, and even humanity's puny ego. Faith in God modified humankind's predicament *and* its structures. The orthodox stressed the predicament modification; the Evangelicals, structure modification. The first interpreted God primarily to provide the Band-Aids or sugar-coating for existence. The second interpreted God primarily to smile at the seriousness with which humankind constructed that existence. This was the argument of section (b).

But there is more to be said about leverage, the essential point under (b).

It was the adoption of the divine vantage point (being one with Christ, surrendering to God) that made the Christian more marginal to the structures he or she so desperately attempted to buttress. Christian's repulsion of wife and children for the sake of eternal life, in Bunyan's *Pilgrim's Progress*, is in the same category as Frelinghuysen's merciless splitting of families and congregations for the sake of salvation. In both instances the personal salvation of the marginal individual is chosen at the expense of the wholeness of families and communities.

Yet it was this bolstering of marginality and individualism that had some unanticipated advantages. The Evangelicals boldly diminished the sacred bonds of language, nationality, and class in order to let real "holiness" come into its own. This all-absorbing sacred vantage point began to function rather similarly to the point that Archimedes said he needed outside the world in order to move it.

The effect of standing outside the world was that one's place within the world (nation, community, family) became more relative. The Evangelicals, as noted earlier, were less interested in associating with compatriots than with fellow converts. They broke down ethnic and class boundaries for the sake of sharing the experiences of salvation. By being marginal to the world they could adjust more easily to changes in that world. As a result they accelerated the Americanization of religion, which the orthodox tended to retard.

There were other consequences of this marginal stance toward the world. The birth of the capitalistic spirit, democratic government, and modern science have all been located in the Puritan/Calvinist/Pietist set of ideas as it began to develop in the sixteenth and particularly the seventeenth centuries. Central to this complex was being in the world and yet not of it. The world was neither to be despised (withdrawal would not solve anything; humans were not any less sinful than their environs) nor to be made more holy (apart from God nothing was sacred—not even the church). And so the Puritans were not afraid of competition, nor did they fear innovation. They had few illusions about themselves or humankind. They only feared God, and it was this fear that kept them on the straight and narrow.

They felt responsible for their actions and thought of themselves as caretakers of God's gifts. Honesty, reliability, frugality, fairness were all values that their faith in God reinforced. Without this faith they would have been less driven and less moral. And because this faith had provided them with an Archimedean point outside the world, they were emotionally free to pursue their secular ends in a purposive fashion. It was the very marginal stance that made them economically successful, and it was their religious disconcern with wealth for its own sake that led to capital formation, hence their significance for the "spirit of capitalism."

This spirit of being marginal and yet responsible was also important for the rise of democracy as a viable form of government. Typical for democracy as we know it is the rare combination of individual independence plus responsibility for the community as a whole. Almost all other forms assume that the two are rather incompatible and that a large proportion of the one diminishes the other and vice versa. As communal order is regarded as a requirement for survival, all communist and most Catholic countries have tended to fear too much individual independence. This is not true for Protestant countries. Both at the time of the Reformation and even more in the following seventeenth century, a new balance emerged whereby a reasonable degree of individual independence was felt to be still compatible with tolerable social cohesion.

The Puritan/Pietist complex of ideas combined an emphasis on the individual standing aloof from, being marginal to, society at large *and* final, unconditional responsibility to God, in whom actually all the major values of a social order (such as altruism, love, consideration, fairness, justice, trustworthiness, reliability, moral integrity) were summed up. In other words, the marginal, ambivalent stance regarding the immutability of humankind's institutions (including the church) was blunted by the solid confirmation of the values underlying these institutions. It is therefore not unexpected that some historians, such as George Jellinek, have found the principle of the inalienable natural rights of individuals most solidly entrenched in New England congregationalism. Other historians, such as Frederick Turner, have found this basic principle of democracy primarily on the American frontier. In both instances it was the Puritan/Pietist complex of ideas that proved to be compatible with this particular form of government.

Puritans in seventeenth-century England have also been regarded as the chief agents of modern science. Why? Some have said that they more than other religious people happened to feel that they were glorifying God by studying God's handiwork. Yet here, too, we must consider the value system of Puritanism for a more comprehensive answer. For in both science and the Puritan ethic the marginal, objective stance above, or at least beyond, the phenomena was central. In other words, it was the nonsacredness of the world as compared with the majestic holiness of God that removed the qualms about rational investigation. Observation and objectivity both followed naturally from the marginal stance.

There is then a congruence between the Puritan/Pietist set of ideas and major cultural, economic, political, and scientific developments in the seventeenth and eighteenth centuries.

CHAPTER 3

Commitment

On Saturday, November 18, 1978, between 6 and 7
P.M., more than 900 members of the Peoples Temple
commune in the extreme northwest of Guyana committed collective suicide by drinking Kool-Aid laced
with tranquilizer and cyanide.

The commune was a refuge from the hurly-burly San
Francisco world where utopian dreams could easily be
hatched but hardly realized. And so 27,000 acres of
jungle were obtained in South America where the
Marxist Burnham regime proved to be congenial to settlements of this kind. Members of the Peoples Temple
in California eagerly accepted the privilege of building
this Guyana paradise where racial harmony, mutual affection, and communist principles were to reign. They
came in the hundreds to the steamy jungle to clear land,
plant banana trees, and build houses and dormitories.

All this was done with money donated by rich and
poor alike. In many cases they sold their cars, houses,
and even life insurance in order to prove their dedication to the cause. Visitors were impressed with the medi-
cal facilities, the day-care nursery for infants and young
children, the class for children with learning disabilities.

People seemed to be well fed and to relate lovingly toward one another.

Who were these people and why did they decide to join the Peoples Temple and the Guyana commune? Approximately 80 percent were blacks, mostly uneducated, in trouble with the law (one woman had seven sons, five of whom were in jail), nearly always uprooted and feeling unwanted in a harsh world. Some of them had been drug addicts who had broken the habit with the help of the fellowship of the Peoples Temple. Others had been prostitutes who through the Temple had found new jobs. Others had been attracted to the food and shelter program for the destitute or the centers for senior citizens. All of them had been attracted by the genuine feeling of warmth and affection running through the entire organization.

About one fifth of the membership were upper- and middle-class whites attracted by the ideals of interracial fellowship and the humanitarian activities. These were primarily professional people—doctor, lawyer, high school principal, nurse, T.V. reporter. They were all idealists. For some of them the Peoples Temple offset a sense of insecurity and inferiority.

This category of whites (particularly the women) tended to be selected for the leadership positions.

All of them, whether black or white, educated or uneducated, had found in the commune the answer to their need for belonging. They were all prepared to commit themselves fully to the collectivity and its goals, if only because their experiences had been bitter, their hopes slashed, and their yearning for genuine, human fellowship unmet. Yet the fellowship, the belonging, the commitments, the humanitarian goals would have been nonexistent if it had not been for the pivotal figure of their leader, Jim Jones. Who was he?

Born in 1931, in Lynn, Indiana, he was the only son

of an invalid railroad man. His parents separated when he was fourteen. His sturdy build and easy assumption of authority made him a natural leader among his friends. He acquired a history of bisexuality and married a nurse at the age of eighteen. He had one son but adopted as many as eight, most of them black or Korean. He earned a university degree in education through night school.

About the time his parents separated he took up religion. Many years later he began his own church by buying an old synagogue in a black neighborhood in Indianapolis. Eventually, this church affiliated with the Disciples of Christ, of which he became an ordained minister in 1964. Before long he and many of his parishioners moved to a slum area in the inner city of San Francisco, where the same mixture of caring for the poor and indigent and dazzling church services was continued. Later, faith healing and miracle-working were added to the list of activities. It was here that the ideas of Jonestown—the Guyana commune—began. Yet it was not until June 1977 that Jim Jones himself moved to Guyana, after the commune had already been fairly well established. His departure was triggered by adverse publicity in the press with which his rather thin skin could not cope.

Over the years his theology had become decidedly eccentric. At some occasions the Bible was called an idol that should be destroyed. In other rambling sermons he would praise Charles Manson, the kidnappers of Aldo Moro, Hitler, Lenin, and particularly Mao Tse-tung. He began to claim that he was God and Jesus. In his earlier days he believed in some kind of reincarnation. Those who committed individual suicide had the terrible prospect of being reborn in the world of 5,000 years ago. Conversely, collective, revolutionary suicide (dying for communism) brought one on a higher plane of existence. Yet at the very end, during the collective suicide, reincarnation was not mentioned. Jones persuaded people to take their lives because the Guyanese army was going to massacre them anyway in retaliation for the killing of Congressman Leo Ryan (who had investigated the cult that same day and had been murdered by some of Jones' followers at the airstrip). He also told them that death was like sleep. In the confusion he exhorted people to die with dignity as becomes "socialistic Communists."

Jones was an accomplished organizer, darkly handsome (he was said to paint his eyebrows), and a spellbinding orator. His people loved him no matter what his theology, if only because in his outgoing, warm, and friendly manner he was felt to love them (he would affectionately kiss any of the black women). Most of them therefore had little hesitation to follow him, even in this last, most gruesome exercise in loyalty.

Death and suicide had always intrigued Jim Jones. In his childhood (very much as in the superb French film *Les Jeux Interdits* [*Forbidden Games*]) he would arrange for funerals of dead animals. He would preach dramatic sermons at the occasion, but the neighbors suspected that he did away with their cats to increase opportunities for the appropriate ceremony. In San Francisco he showed sympathy for those who had committed suicide by jumping off the Golden Gate Bridge, as he said that he innately understood their alienation and despair. In the final hour he spoke of death as "a million times preferable to spending more days in this life." Yet at that same fateful hour he also spoke about the collective suicide as "the best testimony we can make." He had been obsessed with being in the history books and equated the act with a sacrifice for his humanitarian ideals.

Yet the private megalomania and paranoia of Jim

Jones were in final resort less important (and impressive!) than the desire of the large majority to follow him in self-destruction. At the most, 10 percent of the commune members either tried to escape or were "persuaded" by the armed guards. Most of them apparently agreed with the man who volunteered: "If you tell us we have to give our lives now, we're ready; all the rest of the sisters and brothers are with me."

The crux of the matter was that the people had become accustomed to thinking about collective suicide as an ultimate test of loyalty and therefore as something closely tied to what, to them, was *the* redeeming feature of the entire commune: its fellowship, solidarity, and close-knit identity. It was this that had changed life from loneliness, alienation, and frustration into belonging and being loved.

There had been several rehearsals in the past of this "test of loyalty." Both in private meetings of top aides and in mass assemblies so-called poison had been administered. Then Jones would tell them that the potion was nonpoisonous after all and would congratulate them on passing the test of loyalty so gloriously. These ultimate tests apparently made all the members feel proud and even more dedicated to the commune.

And so when the real test came the members were prepared. Certainly the idea of dying for a noble cause was familiar. They mentioned Greek and Jewish precedents. They applauded Jones when he said that he was tired of being tormented to hell and that their children deserved the peace (of death). And when the children and babies, who had first been given the Kool-Aid/cyanide, lay dead before them, they again applauded the man who said that it was better to be like that than to be unable to "grow up to be a person like the one and only Jim Jones." After all, for most of them the last period of their lives had been a happy one and they were grateful for Jones' restoring them to what they regarded as full personhood. To be pushed back to the grim past in an even grimmer future was worse than death, and therefore they preferred the latter.

COMMENTARY

a. Commitment and Community

Successful charismatic leadership and the need of the followers usually fit as a key in a lock. Jonestown was no exception. Psychiatric accounts and journalistic musings unduly stressed Jones' insanity, the concentration camp servility, the paranoia about defections, and naturally, the sexual harassments. All these accounts missed some crucial points. Jones desperately wanted a better world, and his followers equally desperately wanted this vision actualized. Jones gave them the love and affection they badly needed, and he protected the cohesion of the precarious enterprise with a vengeance.

Commitment to the leader was not more important than commitment to the community. They very much belonged together. Instinctively, the members recognized that solidarity was the key to survival. Nothing less than total commitment would leave it intact. Individual freedom was a threat. And so a committee of four censored all mail. All passports were surrendered. Only approved news could filter through. Jones' vision of the collective ego replacing a destroyed personal one was in accord with the wishes of the membership. They were all refugees from a cold, alien world in which lack of direction, purpose, was obvious. The choice to them was simple: alienation without, solidarity within. And they were prepared to accept the consequences of their choice for the "within."

Loyalty to the commune superseded all other loyalties. Personal integrity was decidedly secondary, as witnessed by the self-incriminating documents some members signed. Toleration of sexual interference (particularly by Jones) came under this heading of ego destruction. So did punishment (in the form of public sex with a hated man) for a liaison that had been disapproved.

It was as though the community was aware that sexual expression and personal integrity could go together and therefore be detrimental for group solidarity. And yet there was little evidence of sexual repression and abstinence, a traditional means of consolidating group cohesion at times of danger in both primitive communities and nineteenth-century utopias. Family separation, however, was regarded as not a bad thing in that it removed competing alliances.

Defections were considered a major catastrophe. They spelled successful piercing of the wall around the bastion. They were of the same order as an enemy invasion, infiltration by the CIA or the Guyanese army. They were all transgressions of the boundary, which kept the community so precariously together. Defections had to be avoided at all cost. Armed guards made sure that nobody could get out unless he or she had permission. In California, where defection had been much easier, turncoats were under death sentence and apparently some of them were indeed dispatched.

If all this seems bizarre, it must be remembered that there are numerous examples in all societies of personal lack of balance and alienation leading to stronger delineations (or boundary reinforcements). It is as though communal feeling makes up for personal diffidence. Acceptance by one's group heals the wounds of personal disorder and fragmentation. And so the group becomes precious. In extreme cases members feel that it should be preserved at all costs. Team spirit consoles. To cry one's heart out for one's side cures inner discord. To go all out for a cause relieves anxiety.

Astrology, numerology, and the horoscope similarly provide a pattern when the individual would otherwise feel caprice. Disorder and chaos intrude everywhere. Delineating one's thinking and acting keeps chaos at bay. The horoscope reassures the individual that pattern has won out over whimsy.

Lack of personal integration may entail surrender to the collective. Commitment to the community in turn feeds on itself: In order to strengthen the collective, the individual has to conform more and is watched more. Yet all this pressure can be sustained provided that the bond of mutual affection compensates for what Jim Jones called ego destruction. At Jonestown all the ingredients for the compensation were there: effective relationships, sense of unity, preservation of solidarity, minimization of competing ties, weakened ego strength, weakened family strength (if in conflict with the collective). The crisis leading to collective suicide arose when outside interference (and Jones was quite right in thinking that the commune would not get away with murdering a U.S. congressman) threatened to blow up the carefully cultivated solidarity.

Communal commitment of the Jonestown sort is commonly regarded as morbid and unhealthy. Psychiatrists interviewed about the case assumed that personal integrity was by definition more important than collective identity. The journalists interpreting the suicides assumed that normal human beings would not surrender personal independence so easily. The public at large agreed that this kind of behavior was weird to say the least. For certain, most people in the West happily balance a considerable dose of individual independence with a suitable amount of social conformity.

Yet Jonestown is not as exceptional as people would like to think. Strong communal commitment at the expense of self-affirmation and ego-integration is normal in all primitive societies. As stated in the section on the Australian aborigines, social solidarity was a requirement for survival. In Western societies there are numerous sects, cults, and even common-interest groups where the pressure to conform is greater than the tolerance for disagreement. As far as internal solidarity is concerned, the kibbutzim in Israel, the Jehovah's Witnesses in Europe, and the World Unification Church (the Rev. and Mrs. Sun Myung Moon) in America do not differ that strongly from the Guyana commune.

Nor is the opposite (maximum self-affirmation and minimum conformity) exceptional. Western industrial societies spawn, tolerate, and even sacralize a good deal of rational individualism. So much, as a matter of fact, that it has made the social fabric of these societies a rather loosely woven affair. The meaninglessness and the alienation from which the members of Jonestown had successfully fled are, after all, the inescapable by-products of this loose weave. A high degree of individualism and stress on self-realization make Western societies as diverse (or differentiated) as they are. And this may be all to the good for the gross national product and economic growth, but the latter do not particularly contribute to a stable whole.

Societies with a high degree of economic differentiation also have a high degree of role specialization. That is to say, an individual plays a variety of roles, often separated from one another in space and time. A man may be a machinist in working hours, but a union member, football coach, churchgoer, father, husband at other times and places. What he is in himself as a total person or what constitutes his identity is rather separate from these roles. Jonestown did not treat its members as cogs in a rather impersonal machine. It did not judge them as the sum of segments, but as beloved co-workers in the all-absorbing utopian enterprise. And being involved with heart and soul in the common cause was infinitely better than being parceled out as segments in accordance with various technical requirements. They had generally not done too well anyway in this technical world.

Was Jonestown, then, a nostalgic yet naive reconstruction of times gone by? a restoration of an antique mode of group life? a symbol for the inability to cope?

If one takes the view that society is inescapably moving to an ever-progressing computerized conglomerate in which change and innovation are ever more rampant, the answer must be "yes." Yet if one takes the view that society (whether primitive or modern) is always moving between change and stability, fragmentation and wholeness, differentiation and integration, the answer must be a qualified "no." Then sectarian and cultic movements are seen as staging posts on the road to a new kind of integration. Then communal commitments may even be signs of the pendulum returning from an excessive individualism. Then sects and charismatic movements may be platforms of social regeneration, as they were at the beginning of the Christian era and on the American frontier.

Jonestown was a utopian failure. Yet movements like it may be catalysts or leavens in societies that suffer from an overdose of alienation on the personal level and normlessness on the social plane. In the long run they may prove to have been buffers between too much change in society at large and not enough resilience of the religious and other institutions, which keep things together.

b. Commitment and Charisma

A good charismatic leader provides authority and yet is not an authoritarian. Jim Jones and his followers drew power from each other. He had them in the palm of his hand and yet whatever he said and did fitted carefully with their needs. He guided them out of the strain and anxiety of slum living, neurotic suburbia, and dog-eat-dog bureaucracies. They were stripped from their old attachments and welded into a new community. Jim Jones could hardly have done so if he had been an authoritarian purely interested in manipulating people for his own perverse purposes. It was the sincere and genuine concern for the down-and-outers and the suffering that made him the trusted leader. His authority was accepted because he embodied the principles in terms of which the followers could visualize the shape of something better.

Charismatic leadership always includes a careful perceiving of the times. It also includes an identification with the stresses and strains of the nation, group, or community. Although the good charismatic leader is therefore hardly a foreigner, he nevertheless must have a firmly grounded intuition or vision shaped by outside knowledge or insights acquired elsewhere. Gandhi's leadership was so effective because he understood his people and could provide them with clear goals that had crystalized during his stay in Britain and South Africa.

Jim Jones' leadership was rather inadequate in this respect. The new community was primarily escape from alienation rather than construction of something new. Jones did indeed provide it with a vision of interracial harmony, but otherwise the future of the commune and the deeper meaning of events and experiences were left rather vague. "I want to know that I'm dying for something more than being a mechanic working on all these buses," said the man who was told in 1976 in San Francisco that he would die of poisoning at one of the loyalty tests. The collective suicide was also a recognition that loyalty as such, rather than loyalty to a well-defined and justified vision, had not been sufficient.

Commitment is enduring. Commitment implies emotional attachment, loyalty to a group or idea. It is therefore not easily strippable. If commitments can be transferred easily, they cannot be strong. A charismatic leader worth his or her salt will therefore pay as much attention to the past attachments of his or her followers (however unsatisfactory) as to the new ones. For even the unfulfilling past has its own ties of security, and people such as Jones therefore kept reminding their followers how wrong and evil things were formerly. Again and again the latter had to be detached from the past in order to be emotionally attached to the new community. Religious leaders will paint gloomy pictures of a past full of sin in order to dramatize the contrast with the glorious future. The crux therefore of the charismatic process is emotional stripping and welding, detaching and attaching, desecrating and consecrating.

Charismatic leadership differs from ordinary leadership. It guides change. Ordinary leadership coordinates and preserves the whole. Charismatic leaders deal with passion and commitment, because change upsets the emotions. Other leaders can be rational, because maintaining an identity can take emotional attachments much more for granted.

c. Commitment and Utopia

The Jonestown utopia stressed separation from a corrupt world so much that possible corruption at its own heart was not envisioned. If it thought about corruption in its own midst at all, it was directed at possible defection. Yet there were other sources.

Basically, there is not that much difference between the belongingness fostered by a commune and the belongingness fostered in the world by other groups. In both cases it entails exclusion of others, whether on the basis of skin color or of values. These two often go together. Exclusion does in no way improve humanness. Jonestown expected too much from exclusion. The gradual discovery that its effect on the human condition was rather small was another factor in the experiment going sour.

The Jonestown commune was primarily a refuge for the alienated. Or to say this differently, it tended to attract those kind of people whom the world treated rather badly, either because they did not have the necessary skill or pull or status, or because they were rather sensitive to injustice and meaninglessness. The solution offered by the Peoples Temple or the Jonestown commune was group solidarity carved out from the formless void of fast-moving, change-loving California. By separating from that society they thought (correctly) that some of the values, such as love for others, racial harmony, concern and help for outcasts, could be better preserved. But separation in order to preserve is the essence of prejudice.

This may sound strange and therefore needs to be spelled out. Prejudice is primarily a placing of people and their values in handy, ready-made pigeonholes. If one wants to preserve such Puritan values as promptness, efficiency, individual competition, and reliability and one notices that the blacks one knows prefer leisure, relaxedness, and gregariousness, "black" becomes a handy term to sum up the difference. Blacks who happen to fit the label use "white" as the derogatory word for people who do anything to go ahead with the aid of Puritan values. Whichever side of the fence one is on, the fence separates and consolidates each value cluster. Separation contains and preserves. Prejudice rubs in the boundary line, and those who cross the line may be rubbed out.

An altogether different kind of corruption has to do with utopian illusions. A good system of meaning never gets caught. It must be both broad and relevant, so that experiences and events fit the traditional interpretations. It is corrupt, however, when it cannot deal with emergencies or prevent these emergencies.

The Jonestown commune was fully committed to a set of ideals about life and to ideas as to how to accomplish these ideals. Yet these ideals and ideas did not fit with the facts as they began to worm themselves into the commune. As cut off from the world as they were, the members were remarkably similar to the people left behind in California. They bickered and hated, they were jealous and suspicious, they were ambitious for favors and made distinctions among themselves. Even racial harmony, the main pillar of their utopian platform, was not all it was trumped up to be. There might have been more love and altruism and less anxiety and frustration, but the commune was by no means perfect.

Jones' impoverished, denuded theology was also not able to account for the imperfections within once the conditions of complete separation from the world had been met. Failure was blamed on the threatening phantoms outside, not on his own miscalculations or on the shortcomings of all humans, including the followers. Salvation was too much expected from the here and now. Sin was neglected as possibly fitting the plight. At any rate there is little room for sin when salvation is supposed to be embodied in the very act of living in a commune.

Jones was much better as an organizer than as an interpreter of the human condition. He was excellent on the creation of a cohesive shelter and on the planning of rallies. But he was a failure when it came to accounting for internal predicaments.

This becomes clear when one compares Jonestown with the successful Hutterian communes in North America. The latter have existed for more than 450 years. Like Jonestown, they exclude themselves from the world. They were persecuted for their faith and practice (pacifism, adult baptism) and were forced to migrate from Germany and Switzerland (where in 1536 their leader, Jakob Hutter, was burned at the stake) to Moravia, Hungary, Rumania, Russia, and the United States. Wartime persecution brought most of the communities to Canada after World War I. They, too, are bound together with strong bonds of love and affection. Defections also occur occasionally, and these, too, leave scars in the communal fabric. They own their farms in common and receive whatever they need for daily living from a central distribution system.

Why have they persevered, whereas Jonestown lasted only a few years? The main reason lies in the completeness and fit of their heavenly order (what I have called elsewhere "objectification," "framework of order," "transcendental frame of reference," "meaning-system"). To the Hutterites, this heavenly order covered all eventualities—birth, death, patterns of living and relating, work, marriage, the balance between individual independence and social conformity.

To Jonestown, the center of beliefs had shifted from a heavenly order to an earthly one (racial harmony, loving concern, and communal shelter), leaving the rest of existence dangling. The dignity of individual lives (important to Christians in general and Hutterites in particular), and many behavior norms (sexual ones, for instance) had become trivialized for the sake of these earthly goals. And yet despite the outstanding attention given to the latter, they had remained slippery and elusive.

As compared with Hutterian leadership, Jones governed in a flashy, hit-or-miss, impulsive fashion. By contrast, the top ruling position in Hutterian communities is occupied by the preacher, who is carefully chosen because of his balanced judgment, deep understanding, and levelheaded discretion. As compared with a Hutterian preacher, Jim Jones seemed unable to shut out the Hollywood world and the organizational dazzle and flashy superficiality that belonged to it. If this is so, the tragic mass suicides may ultimately have been caused by the inability to exclude the very rootlessness and alienation the commune attempted so desperately to avoid.

CHAPTER 4

Ritual

Transcendental Meditation was introduced to the West by a gentle guru from India called Maharishi Mahesh Yogi. For a week's wages he promised peace of mind to anxiety-ridden people, young and old. What is more, the Yogi (one who practices Yoga, an Indian system of mental and physical exercise) did not make things difficult for his followers. No abstinence or austerity or iron discipline or inner struggle was necessary, he said, although Yoga actually means discipline in Sanskrit (the classical language of India)—just meditation twice a day.

Even the famous came to the maharishi for help: the Beatles, the Rolling Stones, Mia Farrow. All attended a few introductory lectures and were interviewed. Then the mantra (a Sanskrit prayer formula) would be given to each according to his or her situation. This mantra uniquely belonged to the individual and was to be repeated for about twenty minutes in the morning and evening before meals while he or she rested quietly and comfortably. The mind was not supposed to wander, but was to be brought back gently whenever attention strayed.

The mantra is secret, known only to the individual to

whom it is given. It is said to act like a seed within the mind, filling the self effortlessly with greater security, happiness, and peace. It loses its effect when it is disclosed and discussed in the same way as a seed usually dies when it is uprooted to see whether or not it is growing.

It is the mantra and its daily recitation that, according to the maharishi and his initiators (who after a three-month course in India can also dispense mantras), brings the individual to the transcendental source of his or her thought. Through this constant, renewable link with cosmic order, conflicts, frustration, anxieties are transformed. The guru sincerely believes that Transcendental Meditation will ultimately create peace and justice in the world. If it does not work, checking sessions are arranged so that the mantra can be applied more effectively and effortlessly.

Much more demanding and strict is another Hindu cult that also applies Yoga techniques, also promises self-realization, and similarly has many Western converts. It is the International Society for Krishna Consciousness, commonly known as the Hare Krishna.

The movement was started by Swami Prabhupad while he lived in the United States, in the 1960s. He claimed to be the direct descendant of an Indian mystic who was a reincarnation of the God and Supreme Lord Krishna. It is the kindness and serenity of the followers that attracts particularly young people to the movement.

The devotees follow a rigorous timetable. They rise very early—usually at 4 A.M.—for a four-hour session of praying, studying, and offering to Krishna. After this they eat a sparing breakfast of fruit, milk, and cereal (they are vegetarians). During the day they often continue their chanting to Krishna in a more public way, at street corners. They believe that this constant calling on their Lord (thousands of times a day) is the best way to communicate with his power. Accompanied by cymbals, they most often chant the ancient Sanskrit mantra: Hare (meaning all pervading energy) Krishna, Hare Krishna, Krishna, Krishna, Hare, Hare, Hare Rama (also meaning Lord), Hare Rama, Rama, Rama, Hare, Hare.

Their appearance is rather striking. The men shave their heads as a sign of devotion to Krishna. Both men and women daub their faces with clay to show that the body is only a temple to the soul. Saffron robes are worn by the single members, and yellow robes, by the married ones.

Celibacy is the preferred state, as love can then be directed single-heartedly to Krishna. Yet marriage occurs. However, to prevent the gratification of the senses and to avoid the emotional involvement with one's spouse, sexual intercourse is allowed only once a month. This, the Hare Krishnas think, is sufficient for procreation. The emphasis of the cult is on purification as over against gratification. It is for this reason that drugs, gambling, liquor, and sex outside marriage are forbidden.

Both Transcendental Meditation and Krishna Consciousness are Western adaptions of ancient Hindu rituals and views of the world. Most of them can be found in the *Bhagavad Gita,* a religious epic produced a few centuries before the beginning of the Christian era. It is to most Hindus what the New Testament is to most Christians.

It actually consists of a poem or song (Gita) of the Lord (Bhagavad) or Krishna, who has adopted the guise of charioteer for Arjuna, a great warrior of the Kshatriya (warrior) caste. Just before an important battle, Arjuna loses heart when he sees his close relations on the opposing side. Krishna then counsels that it is his caste duty as a warrior to fight a just war even if that means killing one's relatives. After all, their souls are indestructible and will go to heaven. *Purusa* (the unchangeable, the permanent, the soul, the undifferentiated) is distinct from and yet related to *prakriti* (material nature, change, the dynamic, the body, the senses and mental faculties).

Arjuna is still not entirely satisfied. Krishna then demonstrates that the discipline of Yoga provides the proper perspective on all action, including all that is necessary as a leader and member of the Kshatriya caste. Through the insights of meditation and Yoga one can act with composure and serenity. Passionate attachment to the outcome of one's actions must be avoided, for by doing so one does an injustice to one's innermost being, *purusa*.

Therefore, Arjuna must be united with, absorbed in Atman, a Hindu god, the ultimate soul. Only in this way can he live as the pure, generous, joyful, honest, industrious agent he is expected to be.

Arjuna becomes finally and utterly convinced of his duties as a warrior after Krishna is transfigured into the splendor and majesty of Atman. Awe-stricken, he adores and prays to this sublime figure, surrendering in unconditional faith. Krishna, now back as charioteer, urges him to find full and final release from sin through clinging to him in utter devotion. In the subsequent battle Arjuna defeats his uncle's army and his eldest brother, Yudhishthira, ascends the throne.

COMMENTARY

Both the ancient and the modern Hindu version of religious transformation deal among others with improving personal integrity and with advancing it through ritual. Yet they differ on the effect the social setting has on this process of personal whole-making. Therefore, the commentary is classified under (a) ritual and the individual, (b) ritual and the group, and (c) ritual and society.

a. Ritual and the Individual

Mental breakdown has always been a distinct possibility in all societies, let alone our volatile own. The integrity of a person (whether physical or mental) can never be taken for granted. Death and disease sooner or later destroy our finely and intricately attuned bodies. Anxiety, grief, conflict, tension, change of any kind, and nowadays an almost epidemic sense of alienation, gang up on the wholeness of our personalities.

In the same way as our bodies have developed a whole range of immunizing mechanisms (such as the white blood corpuscle demolishing the germ), so our psyches or minds have erected their own defenses.

Three of the latter emerged rather clearly in the Hindu examples. In all of them a divine order or transcendental source was introduced as the healer of confusion, the restorer of balance and peace. The wholeness of Atman, Brahma, and Krishna (all Hindu gods) stitched together the frazzles of the human plight. Clinging to Atman, taking refuge in Krishna, being one with Brahma made Arjuna a more determined man. Now he could face the perplexing battle in which he would have to kill his own kinsmen, break up families, destroy cousins with whom he had grown up.

The individual soul is another pattern of order, quite distinct from humankind's material existence, unique to each individual and yet linked closely to the ultimate soul, Atman or Brahma. It does not die as the body does and represents the static and the permanent (*purusa*). It stands over against *prakriti,* the dynamic, humankind's senses and mental faculties. It is the essence or core of personal identity and therefore its main defense. In other Hindu scripture the soul is often identified with the universal principle operating in the universe. Yet in the *Bhagavad Gita* it is only once called part of Krishna, probably because its distinctness rather than amalgamation fitted better with the ardent devotionalism of the poem.

This ardent commitment is the second defense mechanism against breakdown. It is the feeling of involvement, a sense of being absorbed in this very transcendental frame of reference. Faith, loyalty, utter allegiance to Atman offset Arjuna's collapse. And the members of the International Society for Krishna Consciousness feel that disintegration has been miraculously turned into oneness through their dedication to Krishna.

Yet if this commitment is to be genuine, competing sources must be avoided. Boosting loyalty means lessening allegiance elsewhere. And so the Hare Krishnas discipline their eating, sleeping, and sexuality for the further glory of Krishna, as all of these appetites can, and often have been, ends in themselves. Even Transcendental Meditation requires that one at least discipline one's thought so that it will not get in the way of the transcendental link from which salvation (wholeness) is to come. Arjuna had to discipline his allegiance to his family and the striving for success, victory, pleasure, and power. Krishna put it forcefully across that all these things could (if taken as ends in themselves) stand in the way of the evenness of temper produced by the discipline of Yoga and "a heart fixed on the Supreme Lord." Only through this religious vision could the unruliness of the senses, anger, fear, lust, hate be hedged about, he said.

Yet there is more to the restoration process than meaning and commitment. Ritual is a third defense mechanism. It makes sure that the bastion of a person's wholeness is constantly maintained. Ritual repeats. It acts out sameness. It strengthens the link with a transcendental order not just by feelings as such, but also by repeated representation. In Transcendental Meditation the devotee must meditate twice a day. Or to say the same differently: twice a day he or she must revive the link between himself or herself and the holy. The mantra must be said over and over again.

The Hare Krishnas do the same on a much more intense scale, so much so that most of living becomes a chanting and praying. All day long Sanskrit prayers accompanied by cymbals and dancing reproduce the sense of oneness, as though it is feared that letting up for even a short while will give the divisive demonic forces a chance to take hold.

In contrast with other Hindu scriptures the *Bhagavad Gita* is not primarily about ritual, but about mystical union with Brahma/Atman. Yet Yoga, which is the means toward this union, is almost by definition a repetitive routine. Arjuna is urged by Krishna to habitually retire to a solitary place, restraining and fixing his thoughts, controlling the fickle mind, holding himself motionless, practicing chastity, disciplining his eating and sleeping.

Yet "ritual" is not confined just to the transcendent. Down-to-earth habits can have a similar effect on personal well-being or sense of integrity. If ritual deals with the reenactment of sameness and wholeness, one can find it in such wordly acts as having a cup of tea every afternoon at three o'clock, getting up every morning at seven, the Sunday afternoon ride in the car with an ice cream cone at the end, or the wifely kiss on return from work. Routines have ritual aspects, if only because they add to, rather than detract from, personal security.

We can even go further and think of our preference for people who are on our wavelength as an attempt to ritualize our relationship, so that the unforeseen can be cut down to size. It is as gratifying to have consensus as it is to cheer for the same team, as it is for the International Society for Krishna Consciousness to chant together. Sameness is reenacted under many guises. Yet whatever the routine it contributes to the individual's sense of being whole, however temporary that sense may be.

The difference between daily routines and sacred rituals is that the latter tend to deal with the more basic securities. The afternoon cup of tea does not help us much when problems of grief or major upsets touch our fundamental beings. Holy rites reinforce the cosmic perspective that cradles our identities. They place the people mentioned in the Hindu examples in a context where coping is easier.

b. Ritual and the Group

As seen earlier, there are varieties and levels of wholeness. Personal wholeness is distinct from group wholeness. Group identity in turn may conflict with national identity. The three examples at the beginning of this chapter each deal with a different identity level. Transcendental Meditation is particularly geared to individual functioning in modern, highly diversified societies. Krishna Consciousness is a tightly knit group forming a haven of security in the same impersonal society. By contrast, the setting for the dialogue between Arjuna and Krishna is a traditional society, where individuals and group fit rather naturally in the social fabric, even though there are profound differences between the values of the Brahman (priestly) and the Kshatriya (warrior) castes.

It is not as individuals that the Hare Krishnas address themselves to their surroundings, but as a group. They chant together, pray together, and face the world together as intentional nonconformists. Without their unity and fellowship they would have difficulty sustaining their values, beliefs, and austere habits. Their chanting of a Sanskrit prayer in a decidedly non-Indian environment is a deliberate way of drawing a boundary around themselves. The boundary separates the initiates from a disparate world. The warmth within accentuates the cold without.

The group, then, has a life of its own. Individuals may come and go, but the community carries on. And it is for the sake of group solidarity that Krishna Consciousness has a program whereby novices become full-fledged members. Only the latter can fully represent the goals, values, and beliefs of the community.

Rituals of initiation guide the transition from the outside into the group. Without boundaries and solidarity these rituals would be superfluous. They are always occasions for underscoring what is so special about the group one now enters. This observation is as valid for the most ancient circumcision rites (whereby an aboriginal boy becomes a man through the removal of the foreskin from his penis) as it is for the various modern ceremonies (whereby, for instance, freshmen are inducted into their fraternity or sorority houses in universities).

These rites are usually called rites of passage; they assist the passing from one identity to another. Initiation is only one of the forms of a rite of passage. There are others. Yet whatever the form they all have in common that they detach an individual from a previous group and attach him or her to another. They all strip an old identity and weld a new one.

The marriage ceremony is a good example of another rite of passage. The bride is detached from the family in which she grew up by her father, who "gives her away," and then the new family is symbolically welded together by means of rings and solemn promises to be loving and faithful under all circumstances "until death do us part." The honeymoon, away from the old family and the environment where one's previous status is still entrenched, is another means to stress the emergence of a separate household that, according to the ceremony, is not to be "put asunder" as God has now joined husband and wife together. As though all this is not enough, the husband carries the wife over the threshold of the new home to underline again the transition across the boundary of one family to a new one.

The same with death. In almost all cultures there are three overlapping phases to burial ceremonies. The first deals with separation of the deceased from his or her place in the hearts and minds of the members of the family and community. Many assurances are given to the grieving relations about the body disposal in order to help them to be reconciled to the loss. The ceremony usually also leaves plenty of room for the second phase—the wailing and weeping—to express the sense of lostness typical for the transition, or in-between, stage. It is at this stage that the irreparable damage to the broken family identity can be emotionally expressed. A common meal is often characteristic of the third phase—a drawing together of the remaining members through fellowship. Eating, drinking, and communing often restores a renewed identity out of the older, broken one.

Apart from rites of passage there is another category of rites that strengthen group solidarity. The rites of passage deal with transition from one group to another or with change within one group. They soften the impact of change. The other rites strengthen cohesion as such, without this cohesion being obviously in danger. They keep the family, community, clan, organization, cult, sect, denomination, caste, class, etc. in operable condition, in viable health as it were.

The chanting, dancing, and praying of the Hare Krishnas are examples of this kind of ritual. Through expressing concerted action they contribute to cohesion. They have a binding effect. By doing meaningful things together the Hare Krishna members gain a sense of belonging.

Caste allegiance in India is reinforced through rules (what work to do, what food to eat, what spouse to marry) and rituals peculiar for each of the hundreds of subcastes. Family cohesion in ancient Rome was fostered by paying homage to guardian gods and goddesses. In China the burning of incense, candles, and paper money for the ancestors strengthened family loyalties.

Again there are modern equivalents to ancient rites. In Japan lifelong loyalty of employees to their firms is strengthened by company hymns and other in-plant rituals. Pledges of allegiance open the meeting of a large variety of Western organizations, such as Rotary clubs, Alcoholics Anonymous, and the Boy Scout movement.

There is another side to the coin. If ritual generally reinforces group cohesion, it also draws more sharply the lines of distinction between groups and between groups and society at large. Religion in general and ritual in particular therefore can also separate. Most cults and sects (such as the Krishna Consciousness) draw such a sharp line between themselves and society at large that they undermine the latter. Salvation, to them, is only within and the devil reigns beyond. The tension existing between Jehovah's Witnesses and many of the countries where they find themselves is their refusal to bear arms and salute the flag.

c. Ritual and Society

Saluting the flag is a social rather than a group ritual. The flag is generally a symbol for national unity, although of course there are flags for ethnic groups within the nation, such as Scotland within Great Britain and Croatia within Yugoslavia. If regional or ethnic rituals are more meaningful and heartwarming for the local inhabitants than national rites, national unity suffers as a result. Tensions between Scotland and England, Croatia and Serbia, the Basque country and Spain, and Poland and Russia are often aggravated because of differences in religious organization or because religious rituals are closely associated in the minds of the people with a particular national or ethnic identity.

There are many other recurrent actions and expressions of values that bind a society together. Similar ways of acting and reacting, repeated preferences for one value over another, commonly accepted customs do on the worldly level what rituals do on the sacred level. The mundane "rituals" or repetitive actions seem to shade over into the kind of rites that are more generally associated with religion.

This is particularly so when these actions and values are discussed in sacred literature, such as the *Bhagavad Gita,* and thereby acquire additional weight. Yet the values discussed in this epic are strangely at odds. Bravery in battle, cunning, desire for fame and power are the values of the warrior caste. Yet not killing, reverence for all that lives, consideration, renunciation, peace, loving one's enemies were the values of the Brahmans and even of Arjuna's eldest brother (Yudhishthira), who revolted against his own warrior caste.

Rituals, then, reinforce the values of each caste and thereby separate the one from the other, weakening the social whole that encompasses them in the same way as the civil war in the epic weakens (actually devastates) the country. Arjuna's eldest brother, Yudhishthira, became king after the battle mentioned in the *Bhagavad Gita*. He was a saintly ruler who transcended in his own living the boundaries of caste and yet also revered them to the very end. He represents the healing of the nation in the same way as Gandhi became the healer of a divided India when he began his campaign to give full rights to the untouchables and outcasts, who were rejected by all others. He called them Harijans, "children of God," because he as well as the mythical Yudhishthira found in religion the source both for strengthening *and* transcending group boundaries.

With all the means at their disposal (whether meaning, commitment, or ritual) universal religions have therefore never been solely satisfied with bolstering personal or group identity but have always also promoted the further (and therefore more encompassing) reference point that could safeguard the society or the nation or the culture as a whole. Universal religions will not only advance self-realization (as Transcendental Meditation tends to do), but also dampen it. They will not only advance group cohesion (as Krishna Consciousness tends to do), but also constrain it. They will not only reinforce a national identity, but will also reform it, as both Yudhishthira and Gandhi conceived Hinduism to do.

CHAPTER 5

Myth

As in numerous other cultures the ancient myths of China mention the creation of order out of chaos. In the Chinese case it was the giant P'an Ku who separated heaven and earth with his chisel; carved out places for sun, moon, and stars; dug out valleys; and finally, on his death, when his body fell apart, formed the Five Sacred Mountains. His head became one mountain, his body another, his right arm a third, his left arm a fourth, and his feet a fifth.

In New Zealand, Maori myths maintain that the original state of the universe was nothingness, out of which emerged darkness. This in turn produced earth, personified by the female god Papa, and the sky, represented by the male god Rangi. Both remained in close embrace and produced as many as seventy children. One of them, Tane (the god of trees, the sun, and light), revolted against the cramped, dark space in Papa's armpits. Together with Tu ("the erect one," the god of war), Tangaroa (the god of fish), and Tawhirimatea (the god of wind), he plotted the separation of their parents. By severing limbs, shoving, and kicking, Tane finally managed to push Rangi upward so that light could penetrate and nature could produce its fruit. The source of evil is traced to this rebellion and separation. Raindrops are the tears Rangi still sheds for his beloved Papa. Not all children, however, joined the conspiracy. Whiro, the god of darkness, hated the separation and did everything he could to hinder the conspirators.

The Chinese and the Maori myths touch on ever-recurring themes: chaos and order are primeval; light and darkness are like intrusion and inclusion, male and female, change and stability, fragmentation and wholeness.

These themes begin to lose their narrative settings the more culture advances. In China in one of the oldest books (*I Ching*—Book of Change—originated as far back as Fu Hsi in 3322 B.C.), existence is portrayed as the product of two opposing forces, rather similar to the themes just mentioned.

Ch'ien stands for the creative. It is represented by six undivided lines and is a symbol for firmness and heaven. It is the strongest of everything under the sky. It manifests itself through change and transformation. It is like opening a door, or like Rangi in the Maori myth.

By contrast, k'un stands for the receptive. It is represented by six divided lines and is a symbol for submission and earth. It supports and contains all things. It manifests itself through comprehension and fulfillment. It is like a shut door, or like Papa in the Maori myth.

Better known are the cosmic principles of yang and yin. They developed later in Chinese thought, at least six, if not ten, centuries before Christ.

Yang meant originally the sunny side of a hill or the sunny, north side of a river, but then it began to mean sunshine and light in general. All of nature, whether organic or inorganic, was thought to contain yang. And so it acquired the meaning of activity, masculinity, heat, brightness, dryness, hardness. It began to be associated with characteristics of human relationships: leading, nobility, bestowal (as the sky bestows rain to the earth). The anonymous writers of the appendixes to the Book of Change believed the number for heaven or yang to be always odd.

Yin meant originally the dark side of a hill or the dark, south side of a river, but then it began to mean darkness and shadow in general. All of nature, whether organic or inorganic, was thought to contain yin. And so it acquired the meaning of passivity, femininity, cold, somberness, wetness, softness. It began to be associated with characteristics of human relationships: following, commonness, receptivity (as the earth receives the rain). The anonymous writers of the appendixes to the Book of Change believed the number for earth or yin to be always even.

More important than the individual characteristics was their interaction. Rather similar to the intercourse of Rangi and Papa conceiving whatever existed, so yang and yin produced the variety of nature and society.

The seasons were a good example. In fall and winter the frigid, deathlike yin wins out over the exuberant, life-bestowing, vegetation-sprouting yang, who prevails in spring and summer. As in a graceful minuet, yang and yin cooperate but also compete with each other, now attracting, now countering, now collaborating, now contending. The Chinese found the yang/yin dialectic at the foundation of music and sacred rites. To them, war strategy was determined by the proper interaction of yang (advancing and attacking) and yin (defending and retreating).

Moral values (such as justice and altruism) were also regarded as the product of yang and yin. Enlightenment in a ruler (the emperor was of vital importance in Chinese history) came about when he had enough yang, which in this context meant leadership, capacity for admonition, teaching, and giving rather than taking.

One major Taoist scholar (Taoism is the teaching of Tao, the molding principle of the universe, sometimes translated as God, sometimes as the Way, or the Path, or Ultimate Reality), Chuang-tzu, related yang and yin to Tao. He taught that both sprang from Tao.

COMMENTARY

a. Myth and Reason

I moved rather quickly from the story in myth to the ideas behind the story. This does not mean that the story is irrelevant and that the essence is basic. In the last quarter of the twentieth century the earlier opinions that myths were not true and were expressions of untutored, sick minds have been firmly rejected. Myths are not any less true than the fragmentation/wholeness theme that is detected behind the Rangi and Papa creation story of the Maoris. Breaking up the myth in its constituent parts or searching for a logical system behind the narrative may actually squeeze out an important element of the truth contained in the original form.

What is the element that is likely to be lost when one breaks up the myth in its constituent parts, when one bisects it as a frog in the zoology laboratory, when one analyzes it (analysis actually means untying, dissolving)? The answer must be unusual. Breaking up a myth is seeking for *yang* (differentiation) in something that is essentially *yin* (integration). Or to change over to another religion (Zen Buddhism), bisecting of a myth is applying *vijnana* (discursive understanding) to something that deals essentially with the opposite *prajna* (understanding the whole). Or to say it in Hindu terms: Analysis is like using *prakriti* (material nature that includes mental faculties) to comprehend *purusa* (autonomous spirit). The followers of Transcendental Meditation would compare the intellectual scrutiny of myth with pulling out the seed to see whether it is growing. For many Christians, the rational evaluation of the creation story of Genesis misses the essence of God's self-revelation.

Still this is not a sufficient answer; this is only saying that some techniques for discovering the missing element are not likely to get us very far. What is the element as such?

Maybe it can be described as a dramatization as over against an outline of the blueprint of existence. It is an account that is acted out. In true dramatic fashion it weaves a pattern out of contrasting elements. It is not unlike quilting. Here, too, a pleasing configuration is composed out of a confusing variety of materials, colors, and designs. As in the average myth, the elements are as close at hand as the bag of outworn clothes in the linen closet. The Maori myth wove a pattern out of such everyday elements as a father, a mother, and children and their inclination to challenge authority.

Yet the pattern represented a new whole, going much beyond the elements or blocks from which it was constructed. It conjured up a vision of light and darkness intermingling and thereby furthering diversity. Or even more, it evoked sentiments of sadness about progress, or (to use again this accurate yet clumsy term) differentiation, leading to conflict and pain.

It is the combination of sentiment and pattern, drama and wholeness that makes this myth and most others more than a dispassionate dissection can discover. There is indeed a building up and reconciliation of contrasting elements: male versus female (opposition), intercourse (union), children (opposition), conspiring together (union), separation of parents (opposition), some children aiding parents (union). Yet the articulation of these contrasting elements as such misses the core of the message. Empathy with and a feeling for the events and their meaning somehow add to understanding the myth.

There are a number of analogies or parallels that make the point clearer. Treating a myth as primitive science or a reconciliation of opposing elements is like pinpointing the counterpoints of a Bach fugue without hearing the music. Or talking about love while refusing to be in love. Or talking about religion without being religious.

The point is important. The analysis characteristic for biblical or religious scholarship generally bores the public at large. What is worse, it tends to claim a false comprehension. Analytic procedures generally lead to an impoverished understanding of myth and religion as well as music and literature. Why is this?

It could be that the tools of analysis (logic, reason, and difference-stressing) belong to a mode of operation that is in many respects contrary (antithetical) to the object of analysis. If the object's primary purpose is to express, dramatize, or integrate through feelings, then cold and sharp logic may be rather inadequate for a full understanding. Much more adequate seems the synthetic (similarity-stressing) mode, insofar as it is open for the integrative (whole-making) and emotional intentions of the object under study.

It is a major heresy to say that religious scholarship is a contradiction in terms. Yet insofar as scholarship is a standing aside from whatever it studies, it adopts a stance that competes with the religious view of the world. As religion—more than almost any other object of study—is bound up with a particular interpretation of existence, it tends to clash with the sacred assumption of scholarship that objectivity and neutrality are primary. This clash is all the more serious in that the faith of the scholar tends to be in the analytic mode, whereas the faith of the religious practitioner tends to be in the synthetic/expressive mode of making sense of the world.

Yet both groups have much water in their wine. The liberal believer is often as ardent as the scholar in his or her assumption that truth and objectivity are one. And vice versa, many scholars nowadays are less sure that the analytic mode is the only valid one. Others are inclined to defend methods of observation, such as participant observation, which allows for full empathy with the religious beliefs they study.

Sympathetic scholarship may (and this is my position) point to *both* the differences between myth and reason or religion and science *and* the compensations each provides for the other. In other words, one can adopt the view that existence is too narrowly conceived when the scientific/analytic/differentiation mode prevails. Leaving room for the religious/synthetic/integration mode extends the horizons. Both compensate for the weaknesses of each other. Or as maintained earlier, fragmentation can be as self-destructive as whole-making can be maladaptive through too much hardening of the arteries.

This is precisely what both the creation myths and the yang/yin philosophy tried to get across: Diversity and conflict may be sad whereas integration and union may be bliss, but both together are necessary for survival.

b. Myth and Sexuality

In the Maori myth, male and female stood for basic elements of life. Just as important, if not more so, was the interaction between male and female, or sexual intercourse. It stood for an elementary process of living. If maleness has something in common with sprouting, giving, dynamism, then femaleness has something in common with containment, receiving, acquiescence, both the Maori myth and the yang/yin philosophy seem to say. Together, as in intercourse, these elements produced something new.

In nature this new thing might be a new season or, to embroider on the cosmic intentions of yang and yin, it might be the balance between radiation (the sun, dynamic energy) and gravity (the earth, receptive inertia). After all, modern astronomy thinks about radiation and gravity as the most basic principles of the universe, from which everything that exists flows, has flown, or will flow. Einstein's formula $E(nergy) = m(ass) \times c^2$ (velocity of light squared) is both an expression and an exact measurement of the equilibrium between these two forces.

One can similarly embroider on the cosmic intentions of yang and yin in genetics. Heredity as the basic principles of conservation and stability (yin, the feminine) becomes modified when in the form of mutation or variation change (yang, the masculine) is introduced. A new balance (or "selection" in genetics) is the result of the interplay between these two most elementary principles of heredity and variation.

The sexual motif also forms the warp and woof of the social fabric. Change in its many guises (inventions, discoveries, trade, migration, culture contact, wars, etc.) acts on the stable institutions (communities, families, churches), thereby moving society in uncharted directions. Our own time is a good example of the attempt to find new balances to replace the old.

On the personal level, change and identity also interact. Growing up (changing physically, mentally, socially) causes stress and the search for a better personality niche. Anxiety, death, frustration, but also getting married, travel, a new job, or a win in the lottery upsets a previous balance and causes the emergence, if all goes well, of a new wholeness.

Sexual intercourse (and this is the main point here) is an appropriate, easily understood image of the interaction between fragmentation and wholeness. It is for this reason an ever-recurring theme in a large number of primitive myths. In all Maori myths—but also in the yang/yin philosophy—nature falls most fittingly into the masculine and the feminine, if only because their coming together is a further apt image of the fundamental relation between change and identity, fragmentation and wholeness, differentiation and integration.

But I have to retrace my steps for a moment. I have moved again rather fast from the concrete "sexual" to the abstract "intercourse." It is very Western to move rather quickly from the substantial to the immaterial, from the tangible to the intangible. In addition, in Western society sexual intercourse as such has been so closely associated with the husband/wife relationship alone as the mainstay of marriage that we find it difficult to imagine that the act can symbolize other unions.

Yet this symbolization occurs, or rather has occurred, in Aboriginal society, where the family is undeveloped as a separate, well-delineated unit. Here wives are made available for sexual purposes in order to cement the peace between two warring parties or the friendship ties with visitors or the effectiveness of certain religious rites. A temporary exchange of wives between participants about to depart on a dangerous revenge expedition or between tribes to settle a quarrel or between groups wanting to consolidate peace and friendship serves the same purpose of sealing the alliance.

More often, however, sexual restraint rather than sexual expression is used to advance an important enterprise or the solidarity of a community. The males of at least one tribe in the Amazon basin refrain from sex before a raiding party, as they are convinced that this will make them more vigorous and aggressive. The same restraint has boosted the solidarity of a variety of nineteenth- and twentieth-century communes. Celibacy of Catholic priests has undoubtedly added to the cohesion of the Church. In all instances, repression directs sexual energy away from physical consummation to greater single-hearted commitment. In addition, it actively upgrades the enterprise, the commune, or the Church as worthy of a higher loyalty than the sexual partner.

Yet the Catholic Church makes also extensive use of sexual symbolism to convey its system of meaning to the membership. The Church is the bride of Christ. Christ is the bridegroom of nuns. The Christian surrenders to Jesus as the wife to her husband. And vice versa, the believer flies to the bosom of Jesus. The Church represents the whole-making (saving) act of God, who is holy (derived from the word whole). It is the disciplining of sexuality that makes salvation as a transcendent event all the more manifest. The spiritual union becomes more meaningful when union in the flesh is sublimated.

Sexual symbolism occurs as often as it does in myth, or more abstractly in scriptures and sermons, because it aptly depicts the pull and counterpull of change and stability (or the dialectic between differentiation and integration). It dramatizes and portrays an absorption of what is separate and diverse in a cosmic system of meaning. In this way change is rendered innocuous. Whimsy and caprice are less final than God, whose firmament overshadows it all, or Christ who took sin on himself, so that humankind could be saved and be made whole again.

c. Myth and Dream

Earlier I mentioned the importance of the story. Here I can elaborate that remark. For in contrast with a structured academic essay the story can be rather loosely organized, going where the wind will take it. Often a myth changes from one region to another or from one narrator to another. It may keep the theme and even the main personages, but the embroidery varies with the storyteller.

It is this spontaneous, improvising quality that a myth and a dream have in common. Both are flexible enough to reflect those elements in one's immediate environment or one's personal experience that are to be woven into the larger, more basic pattern. Both deal with readily recognizable items of the social order or an individual psyche that have to be filed away in the stable tradition or the mind pattern.

One can use the same quilt metaphor that was used before. The chaos/order or fragmentation/wholeness theme may continue to form the basic pattern, but the geographical setting or even the names of the major heroes and heroines may have to be altered to suit the audience. In other words, the quilt patches can come from close by and vary according to local taste, yet the pattern into which the patches are to be woven follows a national or regional tradition.

This is also true for dreams. Carl Jung analyzed a large number of his patients' dreams. They varied according to whatever had happened or to whatever had impressed a particular person on a particular day. And yet Jung found in many of them a recurring archetype (a basic, primordial image; invisible core meaning). In many male dreams he found what he called the *anima* (female, emotional figure) and in many female dreams he found what he called the *animus* (male, aggressive figure). These figures compensated for the missing link in one's character and therefore contributed to greater personality integration. Jung called this psychological process that made a human being into a whole person "individuation." Greater wholeness or individuation, or self-realization, results from reconciling opposites in one's dream world.

Yet myths and dreams differ in one important respect. While dreams relive events and experiences in order to fit them better in one's personal memory banks, myths do the same for the social memory. What the dream does for personal identity, the myth does for social identity. In order words, the mechanism may be the same for both, but the entity to be ordered or integrated is different.

This may have important consequences for the content of the myth or the dream. Myths often dramatize conflicts between individuals, and they are resolved in a fashion most congenial to the culture in question. Yet what is good for society is not necessarily good for personality integration. The community or the family may repress many of one's aggressive, destructive feelings. The myth may act out the fearful consequences of these feelings for social solidarity.

This repression often creates personality problems. What is a social solution becomes a strain for the individual. The dream often compensates for these repressions by allowing their free expression. What the dreamer regards as repulsive in actual life he or she now acts out in the dream. By imaginary enactment of mur-

der or sexual taboo their repression in actual life becomes easier to take.

Myth and dream have a loose and flexible organization around a core pattern in common. Yet insofar as
social and personality requirements are at odds, the
whole-making utility of myth for culture and of dream
for personality may also be at variance.

CHAPTER 6

Morality

Islam dates its calendar from the Hegira, the year in which Muhammad, at the age of fifty-three, had to flee Mecca. The year was A.D. 622, and hegira means emigration or departure. It was the beginning of a new era, the most important date in the history of Islam. It was in this year that Muhammad became the founder of a new religion.

Why was his life in jeopardy? Muhammad had started out rather humbly as a shepherd and a camel driver. On his many journeys to the marketplaces of the Middle East he learned much from the Jews and Christians he met. Later he became a wealthy merchant in his birthplace, Mecca, and it was here that he became deeply interested in popular Jewish and Christian motifs and ideas. He began to have prophetic revelations in which some of the stories about Jesus and the Old Testament prophets became reflected.

Mecca in the early 600s was an important but decaying religious center. It was built around the Well of Zamzam (later called Ishmael after Abraham's son, the progenitor of all Arabs, who—according to tradition— had, as a young child, dying of thirst, kicked the earth at the very spot, causing water to well up) and the Ka'bah, the temple with the Black Stone (probably a meteorite), which was believed to have come straight from the Garden of Eden. Its wealth was partly derived from the sale of water from the Well of Zamzam, but pervasive vices of gambling, drinking, and fortune-telling had begun to affect family and clan obligations.

It was against all these vices, together with the extensive idol worship, that Muhammad first hesitantly, later forcefully, began to thunder. It made him unpopular, so that his life began to be in danger, until first his followers and later he himself stealthily left for the rival community of Yathrib, later called Medina, two hundred miles north of Mecca.

Medina, by contrast, welcomed Muhammad. He had met before with twelve pilgrims from this town and a year later with as many as seventy-five townsmen interested in becoming followers of the new religion of Islam (the Arab word for submission). It was in Medina that the group began to consolidate its faith, its scriptures (the Qur'an), and its military power. It was from here that Mecca was conquered and stripped of its idols.

At the center of this and the later conquests of Syria, Iraq, and Egypt were the faith and single-hearted dedication of the Muslims (meaning "those who submit themselves") to God (*Allah* in Arabic). The faith was the inspiring fire that Muhammad's followers carried as the sacred goad for their holy wars. As God had willed the conquests, their death should not stand in the way. On the contrary: To die for God was to go to paradise.

The faith itself was summarized by Muhammad as follows: "There is no god but God and Muhammad is his messenger." Often this summary was followed by moral proscriptions of idol worship, stealing, dishonesty, slander, drunkenness. Faith and moral behavior were firmly welded together.

The Qur'an (meaning "recitation" in Arabic), which records Muhammad's revelations and utterances, contains more rules. It is explicit about usury, gambling, consumption of pork. It teaches kindness to slaves, respect for parents and wives, charity for the poor, protection of orphans and widows. It condemns cruelty, impatience, and mistrust. The faithful are urged to be honest, helpful, patient, industrious, courageous, generous, and honorable. Those who build up a good record will go to heaven; those who do not will go to hell, where evildoers and unbelievers are fed boiling water and a fruit that is like molten brass and destroys the intestines. As all other universal religions, Islam insists on the Golden Rule (do to others what you expect them to do to you). One is not a believer, according to the Qur'an, unless one desires for one's neighbor that which one desires for oneself.

The Qur'an was established once and for all soon after the death of Muhammad, in Medina. In subsequent years it became necessary to add to the rules and regulations. The result was the *Shari'ah* (meaning "the path to follow," the Divine Law), an extensive system of civil and criminal law, of ethics and religious duties. Some of it seems unduly harsh to Westerners. Habitual thieves can have one of their hands cut off. Adulterers can be stoned to death. Intoxication can cost a Muslim eighty lashes. Yet there must be extensive evidence for the crime, and even thieves can be pardoned for stealing if they can prove that they had no other means to feed their families.

Islam is careful to couch the code of ethics (the *Shari'ah*) in its system of belief. God is thought of as the guarantor or legitimator of the rules. Some Muslims have compared the *Shari'ah* with the shell of the walnut—necessary to protect the kernel of the *Tariqah* (the inner source of life of Islam, the Spiritual Path). In other words, the moral rules do not rest in themselves as the source of ultimate justification; they rest in an overarching meaning system without which they have as little purpose as the shell of the walnut without the meat.

In the entire Muslim world there is at present a renewed interest in Islamic law. At the end of the first quarter of this century Islam was felt to stand in the way of higher standards of living and modernization. Kemal Atatürk's separation of state and religion in Turkey in 1923 was his way of bringing the country into the twentieth century.

Yet in 1979 the upheavals in Iran and the popular outcry against the shah's regime were the products of unease about modernization. The acclaim of Khomeini's Islamic state was a vote for the securities of the religious traditions as against the changes brought about by the higher standard of living and the trappings of the industrial world.

This is also true for all other countries in which there is an Islam majority. In Pakistan, measures from the *Shari'ah* were added to the legal code. In Egypt, there is a ground swell against bars, gambling casinos, and nightclubs. In Tunisia, young students protest against the sexually suggestive cinema billboards. In Saudi Arabia, open antagonism is expressed against those in the circles of the court who use their opulence for license abroad. And in all instances, the *Shari'ah* is used as the base of protests against corruption, immorality, and vice.

COMMENTARY

a. Morality and Cohesion

Drawing together when in danger is an instinct shared by humans as well as animals. When musk oxen in Northern Canada are attacked, the males form a circle around the vulnerable young and females. When Britain was threatened with invasion during World War II, the population felt more at one than ever before; it was prepared to set aside cherished democratic rights so that top decisions could be made fast and carried out efficiently. Concerted action is an effective way to gain the upper hand in a battle or to defend one's side successfully. And for concerted action, an intricate meshing of forces, a careful tuning of individuals, is essential.

Group cohesion therefore cannot exist without extensive agreement about norms, patterns of behavior, values. Most of these norms and values were fully described and appraised in the Qur'an. Gambling, drinking, and sexual license had time and again destroyed the harmonious relationships between families, clans, and tribes of the region. Fortunes had been dissipated by games of chance and families had become destitute. Intoxication had weakened the moral virtues and had watered down important distinctions. Sexual license had upset sensitive relations with spouses and had damaged family ties. And so Muhammad and the Qur'an disapproved in no uncertain terms.

Yet what Islam was against was less important than what it was for. It is one thing to oppose the forces that weaken family and communal integrity. It is quite another to build that cohesion. And therefore kindness, charity, respect, protection of the poor and weak, altruism, generosity, honesty were all vigorously supported. Islam was no different in this respect from other universal religions or sectarian movements. As said earlier, it also affirmed the Golden Rule, which oils the machinery of any community in that it demands the same consideration for others as one expects for onself. It sums up in a terse saying the principle undergirding those social relationships that foster solidarity.

Beliefs are important for the further integration of the norms and values. Particularly when they are strongly held they knit these norms and values together and give them outside, extraneous validity. The Islamic armies of the seventh century are a good example. Their common allegiance to God galvanized them into a unified force.

Beliefs both provide validity for the systems of norms and values that hold the group or the tribe or the society together *and* galvanize them into action. The belief can become a motivating force, the spark plug, or the trigger for the concerted effort. It provides the system of morality with both consistency and its power.

Yet there is more. The power of the Islamic religion in the first part of the seventh century also consisted in the strong discipline it possessed. Muhammad's forces were superior not because they were more cunning in ambushing other caravans, but because they were better disciplined. Plundering meant that each individual member of the raiding party could make himself richer through grabbing whatever brought most wealth and prestige. When, however, in A.D. 630 Muhammad entered Mecca with his immense army of ten thousand men, no plundering took place. His followers worshiped at the Ka'bah and destroyed the idols but refrained from taking booty. The most needy of the followers received some money borrowed from some of the wealthy Meccans.

Without the strong beliefs in God reinforcing the values and norms of the Muslims it would have been much more difficult to discipline the army. The belief in the all-powerful vengeance of God had strengthened the morality of the new religion. It was certainly strong enough to counter the temptation for personal enrichment. It was this very discipline that had so much frightened the inhabitants of Mecca that they offered hardly any resistance when Muhammad entered their city and its empty streets.

All through its history Islam has maintained some of the fervent characteristics it acquired at the beginning. God orders everything in advance, and an austere, disciplined morality fits a dissolute, morally bankrupt age. Muslim sectarianism was a retreat to a cohesive island of order and moral strength in a sea of disorderliness and moral confusion. It was from this bastion of security that successful forays could be made into the crumbling fortresses of a decaying culture.

Islamic doctrine placed order at the heart of existence. Order was not laboriously achieved by humans, but divinely ordained. It was therefore unassailable and reliable, however much disorderliness appeared to reign supreme all around. Islam did not encourage withdrawal from an evil world; it met that world on its own terms. Order depended on a clear delineation of priorities. Gambling, drinking, license were ever so many ways to scuff the very delineations that protected family life and a just society. Sobriety, responsibility, reliability, so the Muslims felt, went together with order as much as intoxication, irresponsibility, and deviousness went together with disorder.

There is a parallel here between the revival of Islamic orthodoxy in the very countries where modernization has improved the standards of living and the revival of Christian and Jewish orthodoxy in North America, where major segments of the population feel oppressed by too much divorce, crime, alcoholism, pornography, and drug abuse. In both instances it is change (of any kind—both better economic conditions as well as greater vulnerability of personal and communal integrity) that one feels should be offset by at least an equal dose of tradition and stability.

History provides many other instances of sect growth

at times of dissolution. Christianity itself started as a sect, a small band of committed disciples around a charismatic leader at a time when the Jewish nation was in deep political and religious trouble. Ever since, Christian sects have acted as oases of integrity and strength for many who felt parched by the inhospitable and dissolute surroundings. Sects have often been first retreats (as Medina was) and subsequent strongholds for the revival of entire regions and nations.

b. Morality and Meaning

Unfortunately, things are not always as simple and straightforward as they seem. A case has been made for morality (a system of "oughtness") supporting the cohesion of family, community, clan, tribe, and any other unit of social organization. A case has also been made for beliefs (a system of meaning or a system of "isness") validating and guaranteeing morality and therefore cohesion on the various levels. Unfortunately, oughtness and isness do not just reinforce each other; they also conflict.

Why? To answer this question I have to retrace my steps. I have said that a system of meaning (or as I have also called it, an objectified frame of reference, for instance Allah, or Atman, or God) contains a blueprint of order, or better, sums up order. It is therefore an abstraction of actual existence that contains a fair amount of disorder, confusion, and dissolution. The abstraction and the deep loyalty to the order it represents increases the capacity to manage or cope with the various forms of disorder or change. I have also said that the ideal order has a dialectic relation (of congruence and conflict) with actual existence: It is different from and yet relevant for life as it is lived.

By contrast, morality (or a system of oughtness) is

much more concretely meshed with the actual, with life as it is lived. It prescribes and proscribes, encourages and discourages actual conduct. It fosters altruism and condemns selfishness, for instance, and therefore contributes to communal cohesion. It also must be specific. It cannot very well say: Take your choice as to whether you are going to be ruthless at the expense of others or whether you are going to be considerate of your neighbor. Cultures and times may change, but a well-functioning system of oughtness cannot afford to take the cosmic, relativizing point of view. If it does, it loses its relevance and its strength, which is the delineation of good and bad in specific circumstances.

The relevance of a moral system lies in its capacity to be concrete rather than eternal. The relevance of a meaning system lies in its capacity to be eternal rather than concrete. The clash between Jesus and the Pharisees in the New Testament was essentially a conflict between Jesus' emphasis on mercy and faith (the relation with "God the Father") and the emphasis of the Pharisees on details of the law. Jesus kept accusing the Pharisees of distorting the faith and the latter kept accusing Jesus of not upholding the law. In other words, the need of the moral system for divine legitimation may corrupt the meaning system by dragging it down too much into the here and now, as Jesus thought it did.

There is another aspect to the conflict between meaning and morality. The first may make the second too rigid and inflexible. A sacred meaning system has the tendency to make everything else under its wings also sacred. The sacred guarantee may guarantee too much. The rules of behavior may become too unchangeable as a result of the divine legitimation. A good example is the Indian caste system. The religious legitimation of the caste rules and divisions up to the present day has made the modernization of India more difficult.

The solution of the conflict between morality and meaning has been to maintain the relation where necessary and to separate where necessary. Islam in its early beginning insisted on maintaining the link but therefore had to make God the author of evil as well as good. The Qur'an, like the ten commandments of Judaism and Christianity, amalgamates God's all-inclusive power to order and ordain with the rules against dishonesty, killing, and slander. Yet, if God represents order and integrity in God's innermost being, and if God is all-powerful and guides the detailed behavior of every individual, as Muhammad and the Qur'an maintained, why would there be evil at all? And why should one be good? The answer was that good works or adherence to moral expectations could never be the final, ultimate arbiter of salvation (wholeness). Most of the Judaic, Christian, and Islamic traditions were clear on this point. If good works or a system of oughtness were the ultimate criterion, the boundaries between believer/unbeliever could not very well be maintained (after all, the pagans were often just as good or bad), nor could changes over time within the culture be accommodated.

This was the vital point: At times of change the Judaic prophetic or the Christian/Islamic traditions fervently affirmed the otherworldly order that stood above time and culture. Any change (and norms and values were more subject to change than transcendental beliefs) had to be made meaningful in terms of what was eternally true. The eternally true was not to adjust itself to the myriad items now on the skids. Therefore, God had to be the author of good as well as of evil, even when God was also the guarantor of the good.

The inconsistency was a logical dilemma, although it was also a sociological necessity. The book of Job in the Old Testament excellently dramatizes the dilemma. The priority of God's being over moral justice sums up what the story is about. Job suffers most excruciatingly from his boils and from the loss of his family, although he was just. Worse was that the wicked prospered. In other words, good works did not lead to salvation. God stood above good and evil. This is why in the climax of the story God reveals the Divine self as the One who has been there from the beginning ("Where were you when I laid the foundation of the earth [Job 38:4, RSV]?"). And Job repents in dust and ashes because "now my eye sees thee [Job 42:5, RSV]." God sums up order, but this order is not identical with goodness, prosperity, and justice. However relevant for the cohesion of actual communities, in final resort goodness and justice alone were not the exclusive marks of cosmic order. Suffering was the lot of both the good and the bad. Suffering could be managed by putting it in a larger context, but not suffering could not take the place of this larger context (God's being from eternity).

The New Testament, too, grapples with the conflict as well as the congruence between morality and meaning. The doctrine of sanctification stresses the importance of good works for salvation. By contrast the doctrine of justification by faith stresses the importance of the relation with God for salvation. They are made congruent by theologians who maintain that someone who believes (belief being prior) will also want to serve God with good works. Yet there is an obvious conflict as well, in that salvation by faith and salvation through God's forgiveness of sin de-emphasizes moral cohesion (through rewarding the conformist) for the sake of healing the breaches of the moral order by forgiving the nonconformist. Instead of punishment in hell or in the here and now for the transgression (which would have boosted the importance of good behavior), the punishment is suspended in order that salvation (wholeness) of individual or community can be restored.

In Hinduism, too, restoration through union with the divine may negate the elaborate framework of good works by means of which the individual can move up the animal or caste ladder. In the *Bhagavad Gita*, Krishna tells Arjuna that the dreary round of rebirth is suspended for those who attain the blessed state of union with the eternal Brahman.

My main point has been that a system of morality (oughtness) corresponds with but also contrasts with a system of meaning (isness). If correspondence gets the exclusive emphasis, the function of distance and relativization (objectification) suffers. If the contrast gets the exclusive emphasis, the meaning system deprives itself of the opportunity to become concretely relevant and the moral system loses its validating tie with a point of reference beyond itself.

Modern divisions within Christianity reflect this dilemma. Within Catholicism the verticalists tend to stress the isness of religion. God's saving act in Jesus Christ is, to them, what Catholic doctrine is primarily about. This is also true for the Evangelicals and the fundamentalists in Protestantism. For the charismatics, too, the experience of union with this ultimate point of reference is the central issue.

However, the horizontalists in Catholicism stress the oughtness of religion. God demands the creation of a better society, so they think. The liberals and social actionists in Protestantism emphasize good works, the dismantling of racial inequality, injustice, and oppression of the poor by the rich.

Polarization of these groups seems to be the inevitable outcome of separating the diverging functions of meaning and moral systems. And yet too much separating obscures the correspondence. Belief can integrate morality. Morality can make belief relevant by means of practical application. It is again the dialectical relation between the two that allows the difficult feat of keeping an uneasy balance between faith (and its capacity to provide a vision above confusion and turmoil) and good works (and its capacity actually to improve social institutions).

CHAPTER 7

Secularization

Hardly a day goes by that one does not hear the words sacred, holy, religious, and divine used in matters that have nothing to do with religious institutions. Some examples:

At a party: "Gladys makes women's liberation into a religion. She is on all the committees that advance the cause of women's rights. She never loses an opportunity to give us fervent lectures on how unfairly our society treats females and how our culture and our faulty up-bringing conspire to bolster male chauvinism."

In a restaurant conversation: "My teenage boys, Andy and Paul, worship the car as though it is a holy shrine. To be given the keys to the family car for the first time is a religious experience. Being in control of a powerful vehicle, having the freedom to go where they like, acquiring enhanced status within their peer group makes them think that the car is the key to adulthood. Andy now has his own car. It gets very gentle care. The enthusiastic discussions about its merits around the dinner table are most amusing. Yet my wife and I would not dare to take it all with less than utmost seriousness."

From a radio sermon: "Hedonism is the god of our

age. Our lives are determined by whatever gives us pleasure. What gives us the strength to cope with the jungle at work is the weekend shindig. The bottle has become our idol because it helps us to gloss over our inability to draw things together. The orgasm has become our heavenly goal not because it expresses a profound spiritual union of husband and wife, but because it tingles our bloodstream. We select our reading according to whether it will titillate our senses, not whether it will help us understand things better. Our favorite television program deals with sensational action rather than the moral lift. Pleasure is heaven, discipline is hell."

A newspaper column: "Our hall of fame immortalizes our sports heroes. It enshrines their feats and accomplishments. Standing before the exhibits a visitor relives the awe he felt for the superhuman strength of the player who made the winning touchdown a minute before the end. It helps the public to quietly remember the outstanding qualities of the heroes who made it to their well-deserved place in this solemn building."

Common room gossip in a well-known university: "Harry is an outstanding scholar and teacher. He is really on top of his subject. Young as he is, he already gets the quotes in the most prestigious journals. Yet I can never mention Freud without him becoming defensive. To him, psychoanalysis is holy. You revere it rather than discuss it. You apply it rather than criticize it. To keep on his good side I avoid the subject. Fortunately, there are hosts of other things about which we see very much eye to eye. As a matter of fact, we visit quite a bit socially, but we have the unspoken agreement to keep off the Freud subject, as it is too close to the sacred core of his being."

Comments by a music critic: "David Oistrakh's inspired performance in Johannes Brahms' *Concerto for*

Violin and Orchestra sent his audience on wings of rapture. As a Moses, he seemed to guide us through the tensions and the resolutions of Brahms' music to the promised land of clarity and final serenity."

From a speech given to a local businessmen's association: "The profit motive is the sum and substance of our economy. It is a Christian principle. As such, it should have our undivided loyalty. We must be on the alert for the many satanic forces that try to undermine it. I do not just mean the communist threat. I also have in mind the ever-increasing red tape that strangles our initiative. It is produced by the human weakness to insist on maximum protection by the state."

A mayor's address on Remembrance Day: "We have heard it often before that those who fell in our past wars died for the most sacred possession of our nation—the right to live in a free and democratic country. It is our solemn duty to cherish their sacred trust in us, so that no one can ever say that they have died in vain. Their death puts a heavy responsibility on us who have survived, to carry the torch of freedom and democracy to the ends of the earth. To renew this sacred pledge is the essential purpose of our annual Remembrance Day."

COMMENTARY

The more complex a society becomes and the more operations and roles become separated out, the more difficult it is to straddle the diversity. Tradition does not seem to be able anymore to cope with or absorb the various norms, values, beliefs, and expectations. The latter begin to hold together segments of the tradition and the culture rather than the whole of the tradition and culture.

Any change puts a strain on existing unity. And yet

the forces that separate or differentiate soon meet the resistance of the forces that attempt to hold things together or integrate. As in a battle, the latter may have to retreat and consolidate the outposts hoping that soon they may be able to reclaim the entire territory. The traditional system of meaning may have lost its extensive control, but it would be premature to claim that now the forces of change and differentiation have swarmed across the field and run amok.

Modern Western societies resemble the battlefield. The traditional system of meaning (often Christianity) has lost considerable ground. The secular seems to have gone berserk and the sacred seems to have lost out. The forces of secularization/change/differentiation appear to have triumphed, and the forces of sacralization/identity/integration, defeated.

Yet all the examples given show that the sacred, or certainly language dealing with the sacred, crops up at the most unlikely places. At the heart of the secular, outposts of deep commitment and holy reverence seem to have mushroomed as ever so many new dragon heads, taking the places of the slain ones.

a. Secularization and Objectification

Straddling the diverse, fitting the dissimilar, is the essence of objectification. Objectification is ordering. It makes order into an object, so that what at first sight is disorderly and disparate can become meaningful. If disorder, change, or chaos can be classified and delineated, they lose their destructive threat; they are transformed into a semblance of order.

Yet order provision also means increased abstracting, transcending, according to the increased complexity of one's world. This in turn means that the abstracted, transcendental order becomes increasingly removed from the mundane and the secular. And this removal runs the risk of lesser control. The mundane and the secular become liberated from the clutches of the sacred. One may call this process of liberation "secularization." I have used the image of the minuet before: the partners (the sacred and the secular) oppose each other, react to each other, but also harmonize with each other. God opposes humankind but also identifies with humankind, frees humankind. Order opposes disorder but also frees the differentiated or the secular through accommodation.

The essential difference between the most primitive and the most advanced societies lies in the intricate intermingling of sacred and secular in the former and their increasing separation in the latter. Increasing objectification or transcendentalization therefore also may have secularization as a by-product. The effect of the Calvinist ethic (a sacred set of beliefs) on the spirit of capitalism (a secular, economic pattern of behavior) is a case in point. The Calvinist ethic encouraged the marginal stance and thereby economic competition, political individualism and scientific objectivity, all of which had a profound effect on the modern secular world.

And yet the separation of the sacred and the secular does not necessarily diminish the one and increase the other. Only crude evolutionism assumes the inevitable progress from the sacred to the secular, from the irrational to the rational, from integration to differentiation, from identity to change. Evolution is never progressive but is always reactive. Change upsets stability, but then new stable forms crystallize out of old ones. And so the sacred reasserts itself under new guises, bypassing, if necessary, the traditional religious forms.

A good example is the attack on hedonism in the radio sermon. A whole new way of life bypasses the Christian ethic of discipline and restraint. It stresses gratification rather than self-denial. It values consumerism rather than frugality. Hedonism sums up this way of living and has its own dedicated devotees. The preacher was right in saying that pleasure had become a new religion. It is a consistent, orderly form of conduct, crystallizing norms, values, beliefs, and expectations. It exists as an alternative system of meaning, fitting a consumer-oriented society.

Another example of a sacred belief that bypasses the traditional religious forms in the West is the belief in self-realization. To its devotees it becomes the major goal, similar to the glorification of God that the Westminster Confession acknowledges to be "the chief end of man." In both instances the belief guides one's motives and conduct. It sums up what living is all about. It summarizes meaning. Whereas the glorification of God implies a considerable amount of social motivation (after all, it sums up and moderates between both personal and social integrity), the secular belief in self-realization lays stress on personal integration alone. The social is only an adjunct to the much more essential selfhood.

The car both symbolizes and concretizes the self-fulfillment of North American adolescents. As the example showed, it stands for personal independence and individual freedom to shape one's own life separate from the family one grew up in. The driver's license or the car key becomes a rite of passage, the changeover to a new "adult" identity where one molds rather than is molded. In addition, it represents a much needed boost to awkwardly lacking power. It provides much needed confidence in one's capacity to shape one's niche in the demanding environment of peer group, social cliques, school, and sexual game-playing. By contrast with the Christian confirmation rite, it is a segmental rather than cosmic order that validates one's new identity.

b. Secularization and Religious Organization

Any organization attempts to protect its own integrity or wholeness in order to better realize its goal. A clutter of disparate objectives does a disservice to each individual goal and therefore organizational separation is often a valuable means to obtain the desired end. That end may be economic (the production of an aircraft rather than cowhide belts) or political (exercising the power to implement national rather than local policies) or scientific (the acquisition of greater knowledge of cell structure rather than the syntax of Ugaritic).

Religious organizations are no different. They too attempt to preserve their ethic or system of meaning by separating it from the very units (whether individual, group, or society) for which it is intended. From the sociological or psychological angle they do not differ in this respect from the economic, political, or scientific. The latter, too, serve the community or the society at large by organizational separateness.

Yet religious organizations have a major problem that none of the other subsystems of Western society has. Separation and differentiation go against the grain of their most essential function, which is to unify and integrate. The distaste that the ordinary citizen has for doctrinal bickering as compared with political, economic, or scientific differences expresses his or her intuition that cosmic straddling, deep commitment, solemn rites, and expressive symbolism cannot possibly allow disunity. Religion everywhere is supposed to be an antidote to differentiation rather than an advocate.

Why then did religious organizations develop? For one, as soon as societies become more complex and communities become differentiated into nongeographical units (such as classes, life-styles, occupational, and other interest groups), there is pressure for convergence of the religious sentiment with the unit in question. As long as the main divisions within a society were geographical (nation, region, community), religious institutions could fuse with these units without predicament. After all, these units were associated in a balanced hierarchy and all members of the community had a similar relation to region or nation. When communities began to be divided in increasingly more homogeneous occupational or other subunits, religious institutions began to face the problem of being monopolized by the one group (or class) at the expense of another. In order to preserve their specific goals (e.g., salvation) from being swallowed by one group at the exclusion of another, independence became opportune.

For another, religious organization becomes necessary as soon as specialized personnel (such as priests and clergy) has to be trained and ordained. In addition, denominations develop particularly in countries of immigration as migrants import their own ethnic religious interpretations and linguistic expression rather than allow themselves to be absorbed into the native, often Anglo-Saxon, ecclesiastical modes. For a fourth, sects develop in opposition to the established churches in order to safeguard those elements in the religious tradition that better fit the marginality of their constituents. Consequently, both begin to stress boundaries and these in turn entail organization.

Secularization has a great deal to do with this predicament of religious organizations (to be separate organizationally and yet ubiquitously relevant). In pluralistic, heterogeneous societies the parts are relatively independent from the whole; they have a dialectical relation with one another and the whole. Instead of a meaning system being taken for granted and being closely intertwined and from birth superimposed on the community, it now has to be voluntarily adopted because of the relative independence of the parts. And so the economy, the polity, and the science become liberated from religious patronage. The religious institutions maintain themselves through internal solidarity and astute organization rather than through a membership that can be taken for granted.

Secularization is generally understood to be the diminution of power of the religious organizations. They cannot any longer ordain or decree their vision of the world, however time and tradition honored. The relative prominence of sectarian movements in secularized, differentiated, pluralistic societies is partly the result of these movements maintaining essential sections of the time- and tradition-honored vision of the world while simultaneously stressing the voluntariness of the loyalties. Another major reason for the growth of sectarian movements in pluralistic societies is the lack of constraint on competing religious organizations. A monopoly of a meaning system (however advantageous for unity and solidarity) does not easily accord with pluralistic structures.

The problem with those scholars who tie secularization closely to the diminishing power of the religious organizations is that they usually wear the blinkers of the established religious institutions who indeed are justifiably obsessed with the decreased plausibility of their beliefs. As a consequence, they fail to pay attention to the vitality of sectarian movements and especially the sacred patterns at the heart of the "secular" subsystems of modern societies.

The examples of religious language outside the religious institutions make this clear. The speech to the local businessman's association makes no bones about the reverence and loyalty felt for the profit motive and private enterprise. It is as though the speaker is saying, "Our economy is unified by this most basic of principles."

The mayor's address, too, is a clear attempt to strengthen by articulation and ritualization what both he and his constituents regard as a sacred trust: the principle of individual freedom and democracy as the means to safeguard the political subsystem. The mayor expresses a faith and he knows that his words will strike a chord with his audience, as it shares the same faith with him. In addition, the Remembrance Day ceremonies and the solemn singing of the national anthem also underscore the unity of the nation. It is a faith that in many of the industrialized countries of the West cannot be entrusted to the religious organizations, as they are divided among themselves and would not acknowledge a primus inter pares even for occasional national celebrations. The ceremony therefore will have to bypass the religious organizations, however much it may borrow from their theology.

The common room gossip similarly points to a fundamental, sacred core that motivates a rather successful scholar. Although the example refers to a particular individual rather than the entire scientific subsystem, it would not be hard to find in the latter, too, a major, sacredly held principle to which the entire community is assumed to be utterly loyal: the principle of objectivity.

Nowadays in the West, allegiance to the principles of the various subsystems does not go undisputed. Economists sometimes question both the justice and the efficacy of private enterprise. Politicians also are occasionally unsure about the functionality of democracy, whereas scientists lately have made some disparaging remarks about objectivity as a golden calf. Yet the uncertainty about what holds the system together has also created a crisis atmosphere in the countries that until recently would have looked on any questioning of these principles as high treason and despicable heresy.

Even in their heyday these principles were never more than segmental rallying points, incapable of fully taking the place of the symbols of a comprehensive cosmic order. This is also true for the many causes that in pluralistic societies are pursued with religious fervor. The example of Gladys and women's liberation could have been complemented with others from ecology and similar do-goodisms. The point is that many of these principles and causes syphon off commitments and loyalties that used to be much more exclusively the domain of religious institutions.

c. Differentiation, Art, and Sports

My major argument circles around the idea that secularization results from differentiation in advanced societies. In the process of bypassing the traditional religious organizations these very differentiations summon quasi-religious commitments to safeguard their own handiwork.

Sections (a) and (b) can be adequately summarized in this way: However long before the arrival of the modern industrial nation there were other social mechanisms that, like religion, advanced the integration rather than the differentiation of societies and communities. I am thinking about the contributions art and sports have made to the sense of solidarity and to the acting out of the major patterns of culture. True, even in antiquity both art and sports came under the aegis of religion. Yet their separation took place long before the onset of the modern era.

Art represents in its many forms what a particular culture is all about. It expresses the hopes, frustrations, dilemmas, accomplishments of actual people in actual societies. Artists think of themselves as mediators for the people for whom they compose, write, sculpt, or paint. Yet what they are the channels for, usually remains vague and latent: as latent as the forces that advance personal and social integrity. Whatever the case, they are the channels rather than the analyzers. They express rather than repress their feelings in their work, and it is through these feelings that they communicate with their audiences or their spectators.

If all this reminds the reader of what I have said about religion, the content of the various art media raises even more the specter of theological dramatizations. The most memorable melodies gracefully produce and resolve tonal tensions. J.S. Bach's music (whether secular or sacred) is always creating and solving contrasts. Any sound is essentially a compressing and expanding of air, and composers make sound-pictures in which strong and weak, loud and soft, discordant and harmonious tones alternate. Usually the final chord (e.g., in Bach's music) is a resolution or reconciliation of dissonants. The popularity of pop singers is more often than not a measure of their ability to be in tune (both musically and verbally) with the longings and exaltations of their audiences. Often they resolve sadness or loneliness by sublimating these feelings in their music.

Similar observations can be made about other forms of art. The best tragedies artfully portray fundamental dilemmas of living, as, for instance, the choice between two evils or the conflict between duty and affection. Like the best-remembered poetry or literature, they often dramatize the clash between change and tradition, cunning and trust, fall and redemption, concretized in persons with whom one can identify.

Painting is an altogether different medium and yet it, too, lifts the sympathetic spectator to a level from which the actual world acquires new hues and colors. Even abstract art, through contrast of shades and lines, conveys a sense of understanding fundamentals. There is a consolation in the perspective of the painter even if the world he or she depicts is desolate, brutal, and absurd. For the very desolation, brutality, and absurdity become modified in the portrayal and the recognition. Or better, they become sublimated and thereby restricted in their destructive potential.

The veneration of sports heroes by broad layers of the population has among other effects a psychological and social consequence. Psychologically, the individual derives a sense of well-being from identification with a powerful figure. Worship has a reflected effect on the worshiper via the object of veneration. The sentiment that accompanies worship has a counterbalancing quality to the anxieties of a humdrum life. The social consequence is particularly obvious when the sports hero represents the community, the region, or the nation. His or her success becomes the success of the particular unit of organization and binds the individual more strongly to the village, the town, or the country.

Most important, again, is the content of the particular sport or play. It is hard to think of a play that below the overt excitement of the uncertain outcome (winning or losing) does not hide the covert assurance of orderly rules. On the part of both spectator and player, plays allow the acting out of primitive instincts of aggression and defense, agility, speed, cunning, swift reaction, skill, maximization of opportunities. Most of these potent instincts have to be checked constantly in industrial society, which in its mode of operation prefers—at least outwardly—civility and decency to brute power. On the playing field they can be publicly acted out.

Yet the chaotic potential of these fundamental instincts is covertly but strongly checked by the order of strict rules. Any game or play represents the situation of individual and society: the excitement of the kill, resilience, fortune, mastery, and ability within the context of well-defined rules and regulations. Stability vividly counters discontinuity, change, and unpredictability: whether one's side loses or wins, order is assured. Or to say it in terms of the bullfight: Chaos (the bull) is conquered by humankind, the defender of order. Plays and games recreate the instincts humans have in common with animals but simultaneously reinforce a peculiarly human accomplishment, a system of intricate rules making for social order.

Religion, art, and sports contribute similarly to personal or social integrity as over against those social forces (such as the economic and analytic ones) that fragment. It is therefore not too difficult to find similar basic patterns in religion, art, and sports. Yet each makes a separate contribution to the whole-making process. Religion does it through sacralization; art, through artistic expression; sports, through the physical acting out of the interplay between instinct and social order. Even if they compete with one another for allegiance, they are on the same integrative side of the dialectic with differentiation and fragmentation.

Conclusion

How can we draw all these observations and comments together in a coherent account? How can we define religion in such a way that it all fits?

Often people have made religion to mean whatever suited their personal fancies or experiences. However, I want it to mean whatever comprehends (not less and not more) the phenomena I have described and discussed. In addition, one must fit the phenomenon of religion as logically as possible in the largest possible context.

Existence is woven of one cloth. At least this is what one assumes. And somehow religion as a universal phenomenon (there has never been a culture or a society without it) has to be organically and consistently related to this large context of existence. This is quite a task. What is more, one cannot be too squeamish in the execution of this task, as the data gap has to be filled with imagination and extrapolation. First, then, the fit for this universal phenomenon of religion.

Basically, the universe can be seen as the balance of the two forces of radiation and gravity. A black hole emerges when the fuel for radiation in a star is exhausted and the force of gravity remains, collapsing within itself. The very pulsating (expanding and contracting) of the universe seems to be the result of the changing balance between radiation (expansion) and gravity (contraction). Force and matter in physics, reaction and structure in chemistry, variation and heredity in biology, change and order in the social sciences essentially follow this principle of two forces (one differentiating, the other integrating) holding each other in a moving balance.

If all this is true, primitive societies advance only through using, modifying, or consolidating the numerous changes that interfere with their stable existence. Society, or tribal cohesion itself, results from the pulsating (dialectic)alternation between change, modification of this change when it proves to be maladaptive, and consolidation, when the change (very much like a mutation in genetics) happens to be adaptive. Families, clans, tribes, and other supraindividual "wholenesses" come into being and are reinforced because they increase the chances of survival of those individuals who modify their aggressive instincts for the sake of social solidarity.

We can happily speculate that in the course of the adaptive complexification (or differentiation) of society a system of behavior norms and values advances the survival of these societies. Social solidarity is helped when individuals are humble and obedient within but aggressive and cunning without. After all, neither the ecosystem nor neighboring hostile tribes are likely to foster blissful lotus-eating. Cohesion and norms aiding cohesion will contribute to greater survivability. So will efficient protection of women and children during the vulnerable times of socialization. It is in these times that learning and modification of less discriminating instincts can take place.

Unification, continuation, and perpetuation of norms and values become additional advantages for social solidarity. It becomes important that they acquire permanent rather than tentative characters. And so the concept of future time begins to emerge. The older concept of place and space has always been there from primeval times, because boundaries and territories already had proved their mettle for the adaptability of the nonhuman species.

A system of meaning in which norms, values, permanency, and institutional arrangements are combined arises as a response to the need for unity and permanence. Death has to be fitted in the system, as it threatens to break down the unity of social relationships and the permanence of norms, quite apart, of course, from the threat to personal physical wholeness. And so death, as all the other "breaks" in the social pattern (such as birth, marriage, the change from adolescence to adulthood), is everywhere carefully absorbed in a system of interpretation. What is more, these "breaks" are ritually articulated in order that continuity and cohesion can be preserved.

Both meaning and place fit in this larger context as ways to advance and solidify the niche of the human species in the ecosystem. Place or territory has the advantage of secure food supply and protection against an enemy through familiarity with the surroundings. Its significance reaches way back into the territorial instinct of large numbers of animals who incessantly reinforce the boundaries around their spaces through scents, bird songs, or frog calls. It reaches ahead in humankind's strong attachments to home, community, and identity.

Meaning, as already seen, is a more exclusively human asset in the struggle to solidify the place of the species in the ecosystem. It contributes to communal or personal cohesion through the consistent interpretation of events that threaten to alter this cohesion or integrity. Time becomes increasingly more part of beliefs or systems of meaning because its change component has to be disciplined and structured in order to preserve solidarity.

So far for the fit of religion in "the largest possible context." Meaning and place are both of the essence of religion; they are indissolubly combined in the most primitive societies, such as the Australian aboriginal society. Territory and social organization belong together; they are undifferentiated. Tribes and clans are inconceivable without geographical delineation. And yet the totems that articulate these delineations gradually also begin to apply to nongeographical social divisions, such as manhood and womanhood.

In advanced societies, place, or identity, soon begins to acquire nonterritorial connotations. An Australian aborigine may think of his identity as determined by the rock where the spirit child dwells that entered his mother's womb or by the clan and tribe of his particular region. Although modern people still have territorial attachments, their personal identities may in addition hinge on occupation or on membership in groups that center around a common interest or style of life. Group identity, too, may primarily be social rather than geographical, even though a community is still largely determined by location. The same with a national identity; it may cohere primarily around a common culture and language rather than a sense of geographical belonging together.

Yet, whatever the focus around which the various "identities" center, their integrity is crucial for their existence. Unless they are a "whole" they are less likely to survive. Religion in all its various forms seems to have always been involved in this whole-making, irrespective whether the whole is a personality, tribe, community, class, common-interest group, social subsystem, or nation. In Christianity the words holy and salvation are both derived from Greek and Latin words meaning whole and whole-making.

Now this whole-making may not necessarily be "spiritual." The meaning system of the Australian aborigines was hardly abstract and otherworldly; it did not distinguish between the physical and the immaterial. The healing of the body has in all religions been part of the whole-making. Amulets, charms, and fetishes are often used for giving the individual extra physical power or strength, even when very often they have in addition a psychological effect on his or her confidence. The rain gods invoked in times of drought are supposed to make whole in the very material sense of helping the tribe to survive even when the ritual has also a nonphysical effect on communal solidarity and assurance.

If religion is primarily thought of as dealing with the spiritual or the immaterial, it is because the whole-making often involved an ordering, classifying, and straddling that happened to be abstract rather than concrete. Yet the transcendental aspect of religion grew in importance only when the culture and society in which it was embedded became more complex. Meaning is not only relating, but also ordering. And when the diversity of the items to be ordered increases, the straddling canopy has to stretch and become more abstract. Order becomes cosmic rather than terrestrial, as the earthly can hardly become adequately meaningful in terms of its own components.

This transcendental ordering people have called "objectification," as order was made into an object to distinguish it from the not so orderly, often perplexing actual existence. Some psychologists call the same phenomenon projection, but the disadvantage of this term is that it has come to mean something that is less true and even morbid. However, without objectification or without a perspective to order experiences, even a primitive culture—let alone a complex one—cannot exist. Actually, rationality emerged from this necessity to relate phenomena, events, and experiences consistently. Diversity and differentiation would have been impossible and would have collapsed as a burned out star collapses into a black hole if it had been impossible to visualize the whole.

Objectification is by no means the only contribution religion makes to whole-making. Vitally important also is the commitment or loyalty to the transcendental perspective or objectified meaning system. Nowadays one tends to think about commitment as central to any religious belief, and for this reason the average person uses religious terms when he or she wants to describe the dedication of someone to women's liberation or some such cause. Commitment is the most outstanding characteristic of the person who was known to be rather dissolute and who has now become a Jehovah's Witness. One senses that the new commitment has unified the person in question. Similarly, one closely associates a common commitment with the unity of the secret society and even defines the unity of the nation in terms of the strength of its citizens' commitment.

Commitment or faith is an antidote to the alienation many individuals in advanced, industrialized societies experience. Yet it was (and still is) just as much an antidote to the insecurity and lack of structure experienced by primitive peoples. The emotional haven provided to lost individuals by sects and dedicated social action groups in modern cities does not differ that much from the sense of belonging and protection offered by their clans to Stone Age men and women. In both instances emotional attachments make up for the threat of formlessness and isolation. If a modern intellectual looks with disdain on this incapacity to cope with what to him or her is the most desirable state (individual independence), it should not be forgotten that any society and culture is built on the capacity of the individual to construct what was beyond the self and, in many respects, required self-denial.

Apart from objectification and commitment there is a third element through which religion contributes to whole-making; it is ritual. Ritual is always repetitive. It repeats a pattern so as to preserve the wholeness of individual, group, society, or whatever the pattern belongs to. Ritual prevents unwitting corrosion by drawing the attention to the object of worship through prayer, dance, chant, song, recitation. It does this again and again. It retraces, as it were, the grooves around order. In this way the object of worship (which often sums up a particular order) will not be lost from sight. It contributes to the maintenance of integrity.

Rites also guide restoration when integrity has broken down. These rites are called rites of passage, because they guide the passing of an individual or group (for instance a family or a community) from one state to another. Birth rites guide the incorporation of a new member into a family. Marriage rites guide individuals out of existing families into a new one. Death rites guide a family or a community from a broken wholeness to a restored one. They strip one identity and weld a new one. They detach the individual or group from one pattern and attach it to another. In doing so they preserve the permanence of the very institution, the members of which are anything but permanent.

When I drew the attention to the wider context in which religion as a universal phenomenon could be placed, I stressed the dialectic between wholeness and fragmentation in nature and life as well as in culture and society. If religion is on the whole-making side of this dialectic, as I have suggested, it cannot very well maintain itself unless it is constantly on the alert for the potential of change and fragmentation. After all, fragmentation is the universal principle underlying the ability to improve humankind's niche in the ecosystem. And no amount of whole-making is likely to prevent the vigorous prospering of whatever advances the better fit or the better mastery of nature.

Not all change is for the good, and so a viable religion becomes very discerning as to which kinds of change must be encouraged and guided and which kinds of change should be discouraged. The rites of passage are a good example of the kind of change that is guided by ritual in order to preserve the identity of individual or group likely to be suffering from the change. Conversion and charismatic leadership are two other ways religion uses to guide change. As seen in chapter 2, the Evangelicals and the Pietists used to great advantage their ability to strip persons from inadequate identities in order to weld them to better-fitting ones. Their charismatic leaders similarly stripped groups from their ethnic or class identities and welded them into new communities.

In order to discern which change is good and which change is bad, religion must have a criterion, preferably one that has withstood the onslaught of time and place; its meaning system usually incorporates such a criterion. And so the social activists in Christian churches devote themselves to greater justice for the unprivileged and the powerless, because they perceive their ideal order to contain clear criteria for justice. Therefore, Christian beliefs do not just generally reinforce the status quo or a social identity, they also provide the status quo with the otherworldly criteria in terms of which its corruption or fragmentation can be healed.

The fourth element by means of which religion contributes to whole-making incorporates another way of dealing with change so that it can be disciplined. Ancient myths or more up-to-date theological systems often dramatize the conflict between wholeness and fragmentation or identity and change. This acting out of basic dilemmas of individuals, groups, and societies is not just a peculiarly religious interest; art and play similarly integrate communities through dramatizing conflicts between order and aggression, tradition and change, rules and mastery.

Myths and theology have their own way of reenacting the dialectic between wholeness and fragmentation. They often put the contrast in supernatural terms. The god of heaven interacts with the god of earth. Or the powers of light intrude on the powers of darkness. Or the savior conquers sin. Or life is born out of death, the resurrection follows the crucifixion. The basic theme is usually hidden in a changing account. The novelty of combining and recombining the materials close at hand (a bird, a father, a mother, a child, thunder and lightning) is disciplined by the enacted, often latent rather than articulated theme.

Many times the truth expressed by ancient myths or theology goes deeper than the different kind of truth of logical evidence and causal relations. The former is generally much more fundamental and has an emotional/aesthetic quality the latter misses. Scientific truth also confines itself strictly to the segments of research where rational, analytical procedures can be applied. For this reason it is also less interested in synthetic modes that concentrate on the whole, even when it assumes the existence of order as ardently as the worshiper. Because religion deals with ordering and whole-making it tends to also be rather adept at locating those regions where the potential for disorder is considerable. These regions may be called "sin" or the flawedness and brokenness of existence. More often they are pinpointed specifically, such as when a government is called unjust, trade practices are condemned as corrupt, or individuals are deemed selfish and overbearing.

Moral prescriptions and proscriptions may be legitimated by religion, but if religion does not also occupy itself with a more cosmic, wider meaning, it may succumb to the momentariness of the causes it condemns or encourages. John Oman put it rather well when he said that religion without morality lacked a solid earth to walk on and that morality without religion lacked a wide heaven to breathe in. They (religion and morality) are dialectically related rather similarly as Rangi, the sky god, was related to his wife, Papa, the earth god, in an ancient Maori myth. They have their separate domains, but they also interact.

Differentiation and dialectic have become rather salient terms in this account. Religion and morality have become separated out (differentiated) in industrial, urbanized societies. Yet they maintain a dialectic relation of complementing and contending. This is also true for the relation between religion and the economic, political, education, and scientific subsystems in these same societies. Religious institutions compete with the not-very-successful sacralizing tendencies within these subsystems. Because the feeble sacralizations of the secular structures are segmental, the traditional religious meaning systems complement with their comprehensive, cosmic vision of order.

On this level of cosmic ordering the sectarian/evangelical segment of the broad theological spectrum in industrialized, urbanized societies has an advantage reflected in its present expansion and ebullience. It combines a high level of commitment with a clear delineation of its traditional beliefs. It meets a secular insipidness and cynical wishy-washiness head on with a forceful set of affirmations. One of these is infallibility (papal for Catholics, scriptural for Protestants). Another one is a clear outline of the past (God's revelation in Jesus Christ) and usually a concrete expectation of the future (Christ's return in glory or the Armageddon). A third one is an uninhibited view of the concreteness of sin and a just as solid belief in the actuality of redemption and salvation.

All these views are much less central, if not implausible, in the liberal, rationalistic segment of the theological spectrum. Its defense of salvation being essentially humankind's work, its alliance with an embattled humanism, its deification of self-realization in accordance with the decreasing plausibility of individual rationalism as the acme of creation, somehow seem to have become less reasonable, taken for granted, and hollower.

It all makes sense in terms of our dialectical assumptions. At times of insecurity and rampant change those cosmic delineations that postulate order at the heart of history will make more converts than the vague confusions of those existential segments that rely on scientific proof. This will be all the more so when these delineations are more than mere musings and are solidly entrenched in the deep commitments of communities of believers. For it is in sentiments of loyalty and faith that integration usually comes to its fullest flower.

How can this account be summed up in one short paragraph? From the social scientific perspective (only one perspective among many possible others), religion can be fittingly regarded as the sacralization of identity. After all, in the social sciences the problem of how individuals, groups, and societies hang together is the central problem and this definition of religion addresses itself to this problem. Now these "identities" are not necessarily congruent; actually, they often conflict. Yet religion generally modifies these conflicts even when it also reinforces each identity level separately. Sacralization can be best defined as practically consisting of (a) objectification (transcendental ordering), (b) commitment (emotional anchoring), (c) ritual (sameness enacting), and (d) myth (dialectic dramatization). These four elements do not necessarily all have to be present for the process to be sacralizing. Yet if too few are present, it would be difficult to maintain that we observe a religious phenomenon; if all are present, we can be certain that the public will call the phenomenon "religious."

SUGGESTED READINGS

Chapter 1 **Place**

Berndt, Ronald M. "Traditional Morality as Expressed Through the Medium of an Australian Aboriginal Religion" in Berndt, Ronald M., ed., *Australian Aboriginal Anthropology*. Nedlands, West Australia: University of Western Australia Press, 1970, pp. 216–47.

Mol, Johannis (Hans) J. *The Firm and the Formless* (Religion and Identity in Aboriginal Australia). Waterloo, Ont.: Wilfrid Laurier University Press, 1982.

———. "The Origin and Function of Religion: A Critique of, and Alternative to, Durkheim's Interpretation of the Religion of Australian Aborigines," *Journal for the Scientific Study of Religion*, Vol. 18, No. 4 (December 1979), pp. 379–89.

Chapter 2 **Meaning**

Bellah, Robert N. *Beyond Belief.* New York: Harper & Row, 1970.

Mol, Johannis (Hans) J. *The Breaking of Traditions.* Berkeley, CA: Glendessary Press, 1968.

———. *Identity and the Sacred.* Oxford: Blackwell, 1976; New York: Free Press, 1977, chapters 2, 3, and 9.

Chapter 3 **Commitment**

Kanter, Rosabeth Moss. *Commitment and Community.* Cambridge, MA: Harvard University Press, 1972.

Keniston, Kenneth. *The Uncommitted.* New York: Harcourt Brace Jovanovich, 1964.

Mol, Johannis (Hans) J. *Identity and the Sacred.* Oxford: Blackwell, 1976; New York: Free Press, 1977, chapters 4 and 15.

Chapter 4 **Ritual**

Durkheim, Emile. *Elementary Forms of Religious Life.* Glencoe, IL: Free Press, 1954; first published, 1912.

Mol, Johannis (Hans) J. *Identity and the Sacred.* Oxford: Blackwell, 1976; New York: Free Press, 1977, chapter 16.

Needleman, Jacob. *The New Religions.* Garden City, NY: Doubleday, 1970.

Chapter 5 **Myth**

Jung, Carl G. *Psychology and Religion.* New Haven, CT: Yale University Press, 1972; first published, 1938.

Mol, Johannis (Hans) J. *The Fixed and the Fickle* (Religion and Identity in New Zealand). Waterloo, Ont.: Wilfrid Laurier University Press, 1982.

————. *Identity and the Sacred.* Oxford: Blackwell, 1976; New York: Free Press, 1977, chapter 17.

Chapter 6 **Morality**

Gibb, H.A.R. *Mohammedanism.* New York: Mentor Books, 1953.

Mol, Johannis (Hans) J. "Belief: Its Contribution to Wholemaking," *Religious Traditions* (A Journal in the Study of Religion), Vol. 2, No. 2 (October 1979), pp. 6–23.

————. *Christianity in Chains.* Melbourne: Nelson, 1969, chapters 1 and 6.

Chapter 7 **Secularization**

Martin, David. *A General Theory of Secularization.* Oxford: Blackwell, 1978.

Mol, Johannis (Hans) J. "Introduction" in Hans Mol, ed., *Identity and Religion*. London: Sage, 1978, pp. 1–17.

———. *Wholeness and Breakdown (A Model for the Interpretation of Nature and Society)*. Madras: Dr. S. Radhakrishnan Institute for Advanced Study in Philosophy, University of Madras, 1978.

GLOSSARY

The emphasis is not on strict definitions, but on approximate explanations whenever the term is found in the text.

adaptation   alteration to fit; making suitable

alienation   whatever prevents integration and wholeness; sense of feeling estranged, an alien, rootless; isolation from others

anomie   lack of control by the group over its members; disorganization of personal values as a result of stress; lack of clear-cut guide about the rules, expectations, and ideas of a society

archetype   a basic, primordial image; an invisible core meaning

Bhagavad Gita **(Hinduism)**   epic poem dealing with the song (Gita) of the Lord Krishna (Bhagavad = Lord); at least 2,000 years old

bureaucracy   a type of organization characterized by formal rules, specialized tasks, and impersonal contacts

catalyst   a person or chemical initiating a reaction or speeding up a reaction; causing a change from old ways to new ways

cathexis   investment of emotion in an object

charisma   the process by which a group or society is stripped from an old identity and welded to a new one; facilitates detachment from old ways and attachment to new ones; the force that welds together a group or society in a common purpose

ch'ien (Chinese)   the creative; firmness; heaven

cohesion   sticking together

commitment   emotional involvement or attachment; attachments of feelings to an identity or system of meaning; being pledged to a position; loyalty to a cause

concretization   the process of making concrete, seen, heard, or tasted; making something abstract applicable; making an idea or belief concrete or visible

conversion   a turning or a change from one set of beliefs to another; change from one identity to another

dialectic   the conflicting and complementing of opposing forces; a tug-of-war, a seesaw, a teeter-totter relationship; pull and counterpull between forces that need and oppose each other (for instance, progress and order)

differentiation   what makes for change and more variety; the formation of differences and specialization; the development of various "un"-like opinions, meanings, ideas, and functions; a continuous specialization of tasks; fragmentation

dominance hierarchy   the ranking of individuals according to the power they possess

Dreaming (The)   the representation of a larger order in Australian aboriginal society. It combines many items that the Western mind strictly separates: reality, symbol, body, spirit, totem, spirit-site

dysfunction   something has a dysfunction for something else if it is of disadvantage to the latter; disrupting relationships

evolution   compromise between sameness and change; not as rigid as sameness and not as rapidly shifting as change

function   something has a function for something else if it is of advantage to the latter; serving relationships

identity   a stable niche in a predictable environment; that which makes an individual, group, or society whole; accumulated confidence in one's ability to maintain inner sameness, internal unity; a stable setting within whose boundaries an individual or group can find order and sameness; the place into which an individual, group, or society fits; the core group of beliefs, values, and ideas of an individual or society; if it refers to space, the vernacular sometimes calls it "one's turf"

individuation (Jungian psychology) whole-making of a person; personality integration

integration what binds together; maintaining sameness; making something whole or one; strengthening a system from within; a binding together; an abiding concern with wholeness, unity, and order

interpretation of reality explaining, translating, clarifying what the world around oneself is all about; unraveling the meaning of the real

k'un (Chinese) the receptive; submission; earth

legitimation making legal or lawful

liminality literally "being on the threshold"; the transitional stage between an old identity and a new one; the in-between stage; being on the boundary

mantra (Hinduism) prayer formula—almost always in Sanskrit

marginality being at the periphery or on the edge; being on the outside of things; existing on the border of things neither completely accepted nor rejected by others

meaning making sense of one's world; understanding life and feeling at home in that world; the sense of a word or event in relation to something else; the end purpose or significance of something; relating experiences and events to a larger context

moiety usually the exogamous half of a tribe; the half of a tribe providing the marriage partners for the other half

morality system of norms and values determining the rightness or wrongness of an action; rules of behavior

myth the outlook and experience of a society distilled into a symbolic story form; a shared set of symbols; a way to interpret reality; tying present experiences to past events; a belief or statement of a person's place in his or her environment

objectification an overall theory or world view that works as a standard by which to judge the world; making order into an object, thereby relativizing mundane disorder and change; the projection of meaning and order into a transcendent point of reference; the creation of meaning for the here and now; a platform of confidence outside the world, through which change can be accepted

objectivity   ability to stand outside the phenomena one analyzes or judges

order   pattern; fixed routine; uniform system; the opposite of chaos

otherness   being different and opposite; being beyond time or place

pluralism   a situation in which there are many options for choice and many systems of meaning

postliminality   literally "being over the threshold"; being in the process of acquiring a new identity or status; the welding of a new identity; being attached to a new identity; being past the boundary

prajna (Zen Buddhism)   understanding the whole

prakriti (Hinduism)   material nature; change; the dynamic; the body; the senses and mental faculties

preliminality   literally "being before the threshold"; being in the process of giving up an old identity; the stripping of an old identity; being detached from an old identity; being before the boundary

purusa (Hinduism)   the unchangeable; the permanent; the undifferentiated; the soul

rationalism   system of thought based on logical consistency and reason

relevance   being associated with or applicable to a problem or topic

rigidification   making something inflexible, rigid

rites of passage   rituals dealing with passing from one identity to another (such as birth, initiation, marriage, death)

ritual   a routinized way of doing things; regular, customary observance or practice

sacralization   reinforcing, protecting by means of objectification, commitment, ritual, or myth; making sacred; one way to strengthen integration

sect   a group holding religious opinions different from the usual

security   feeling free of danger, fear; feeling free and protected; confidence in not failing or becoming lost

shaman   usually a witchdoctor with charismatic influence who informs the community about the supernatural world and who engages in faith-healing

Shari'ah   divine law of Islam

subsystem   a system (e.g., a religious group) within a system (e.g., a society)

synthesis   process of combining ideas

Tariqah   spiritual source of life of Islam

transcendence   that which lies beyond the limits of experience

vijnana (Zen Buddhism)   discursive understanding

yang (Chinese)   the sunny side of a hill; activity; masculinity; hardness

yin (Chinese)   the dark side of a hill; passivity; femininity; softness

Yoga   an Indian system of mental and physical exercise

Yogi   a person who practices Yoga